D1530903

WHAT A YEAR IT WAS!

1949

A walk back in time to revisit what life was like in the year that has special meaning for you...

Congratulations
and
Best Wishes

To

From

DEDICATION

To Danielle...
The Joy And Love You Bring To My Life Is More
Than I Ever Could Have Imagined.
You Are, Indeed, A Great Blessing...

Designers • Peter Hess & Marguerite Jones
Research and Special Segments Writer • Laurie Cohn

Inquiries should be addressed to:
MMS Publishing, 5429 McConnell Avenue, Los Angeles, California 90066.
Printed and bound in the United States.

CONTENTS

POLITICS and WORLD EVENTS

HARRY S. TRUMAN Sworn In As 33rd President Of The United States

In the first televised inauguration, which is carried as far west as Sedalia, Missouri, 20 million people — more than all previous inaugurations combined — watch as President Truman is sworn in and outlines his four-point program supporting the United Nations, world trade and denouncement of communism.

President Truman makes address at State dinner.

1949

Europe's Starving

Chairman of the C.A.R.E. committee, DOUGLAS FAIRBANKS, JR., is greeted warmly as he visits a refugee camp in Greece.

Nowhere in Europe are the effects of malnutrition more pathetically apparent.

Children

Mr. Fairbanks observes firsthand just how desperately needed are the food packages being sent to Europe through his organization.

Religious groups are attempting to care for more than 5,000 people.

The arrival of C.A.R.E. packages is the one bright ray of hope in the struggle for survival.

These youngsters are particularly happy as there's chocolate in this package – a favorite of kids anywhere in the world.

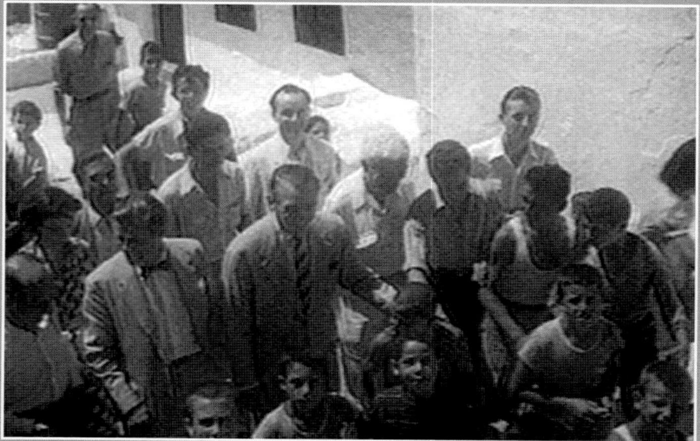

Mr. Fairbanks encourages the world to "Share With C.A.R.E." as hunger knows no nationality.

1949

THE BERLIN AIRLIFT BRINGS FOOD RELIEF

Workers put up a new sign.

After the reds capitulate lifting the Berlin blockade, trucks take up the job of feeding the city that had survived through the raw courage of airmen who kept supplies coming.

Delighted citizens wave as the trucks carrying food and supplies drive to their destination.

1949 ADVERTISEMENT

Extra Pleasure • Extra Comfort • No Extra Fare

"Scenic way" is *right!* Only the amazing new California Zephyr gives you the *double* thrill of riding the most wonderful train in the world right *through* America's most wonderful scenery. And *what* a way to see it! The new VISTA-DOME way! *Now* you can look ahead... look up... look down... look *everywhere*... while you glide in luxurious comfort through the magnificent Colorado Rockies and Feather River Canyon in daylight hours... Utah and Nevada by starlight or moonlight. Your choice of low cost VISTA-DOME reclining chair coaches or new type Pullman accommodations, drawing rooms, bedrooms, roomettes and sections. Through sleeper daily between New York and San Francisco.

NEW, FASTER DAILY SCHEDULES

WESTBOUND (Read Down)		EASTBOUND (Read Up)
3:30 PM Lv	Chicago	Ar 1:30 PM
11:59 PM Lv	Omaha	Ar 4:55 AM
1:19 AM Lv	Lincoln	Ar 3:40 AM
8:40 AM Lv	Denver	Ar 7:00 PM
	Colorado Rockies	
1:53 PM Lv	Glenwood Springs	Lv 1:35 PM
10:25 PM Lv	Salt Lake City	Lv 5:40 AM
	Feather River	
7:00-11:00 AM	**Canyon**	2:00-6:00 PM
12:28 PM Lv	Sacramento	Lv 12:50 PM
1:34 PM Ar	Stockton	Lv 11:53 AM
4:00 PM Ar	Oakland	Lv 9:44 AM
4:50 PM Ar	San Francisco	Lv 9:00 AM

BURLINGTON • RIO GRANDE • WESTERN PACIFIC

A NEW STATE IS BORN

BONN REPUBLIC

Konrad Adenauer *(left)* is the new chancellor of the Bonn Republic and Theodor Heuss its president.

Under a new banner pledged to oppose communism the new Republic takes its place in the community of free nations.

Yugoslavia

Within the communist ranks, the voice of rebellion is heard as Yugoslavia's Marshall Tito turns on his Kremlin masters.

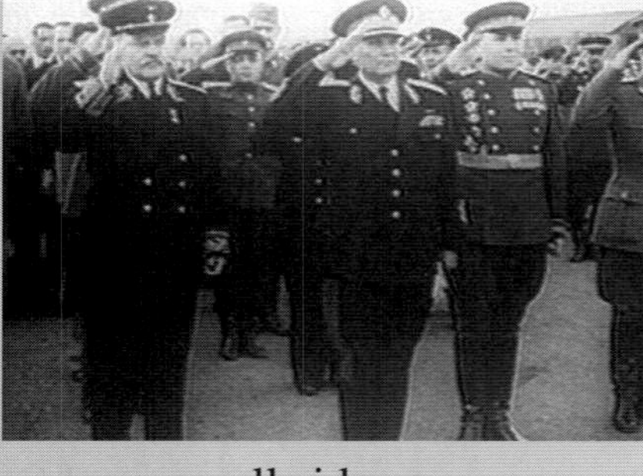

Tito, pictured with his former Russian buddies, now faces the full fury of Soviet revenge on all sides.

Yugoslavia is turned into an armed camp ready for a fight to the finish.

THE WAR ON COMMUNISM IS FOUGHT ON MANY FRONTS

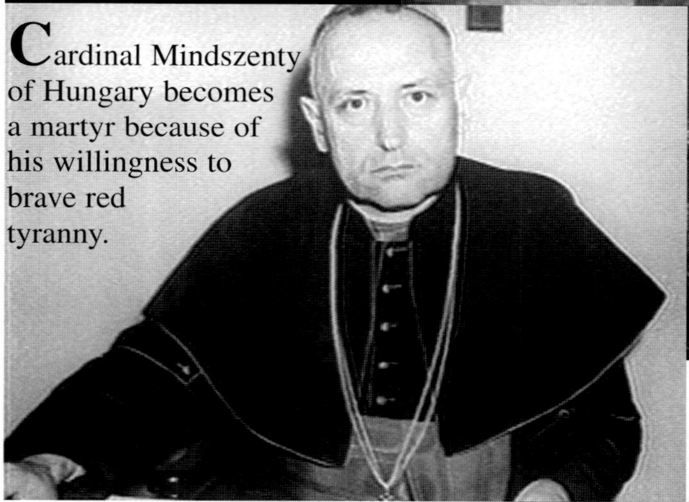

Cardinal Mindszenty of Hungary becomes a martyr because of his willingness to brave red tyranny.

Under the leadership of Pope Pius, churches throughout the world join in protesting the life imprisonment of a churchman.

Crowds gather in Rome to pray for the Cardinal's release.

1949 COMMUNISM MAKES FORMIDABLE GAINS IN CHINA

Shanghai's fall is but one in an unbroken string of victories.

Red armies overrun almost the entire continental mass of China.

As the year ends Chiang Kai-shek and his demoralized government flee to the island of Formosa while the red banner flag floats triumphantly over 400 million people.

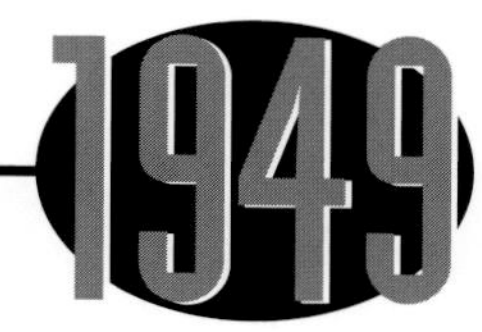

CHINA

A New Red Flag With Five Yellow Stars Flies Over Square Of The Gate Of Heavenly Peace In Peiping - Renamed Peking.

PEKING

Chinese Communists Seize Control Of Peking.

NANKING

Communists Surround Shanghai.

SHANGHAI

YANGTZE R.

Chinese Communist Troops Occupy Nationalist China Former Capital Of Canton.

FORMOSA

Mao Tse-tung Establishes Communist People's Republic of China With Chou En-lai Appointed Premier.

Mao Appoints Regime North Of Yangtze.

Under Orders From Mao, One Million Men Launch Major Offensive Across The Yangtze River To "Liberate" China.

Chiang Kai-shek

Resigns As President Of China – Relocates Forces To Formosa.

SUPREME WAR COUNCIL IS FORMED UNDER NATIONALIST CHIANG KAI-SHEK.

Nationalist Chinese Shell U.S. Ship "Flying Cloud" In Coastal Blockade.

Representatives Of Tibet's 15-Year Old Dalai Lama's Ruling Regime Send Message To The United States Begging For Protection From Communist China.

Save Tibet

Tientsin Falls To Reds After Intense Battle.

U.S. BARS ADDITIONAL AID TO NATIONALIST CHINA BLAMING COLLAPSE OF CHINA ON CORRUPTION IN CHIANG KAI-SHEK REGIME.

Communist Peace Ultimatum Rejected In Nanking.

1949

Acting president of Nationalist China Li Sung-jen is given a floral greeting as he arrives in New York for medical treatment. During his absence Chiang Kai-shek resumes leadership.

PARIS

Is The Site For Delegates From Western Europe And The United States To Meet To Draft A Common Defense Program.

General **Omar Bradley** is one of the representatives from the United States.

Secretary of Defense **Louis Johnson** *(far left)* takes a leading role at the conference, as does United States Emissary **Averell Harriman** *(right)*, but the approval of the agreement as far as American military aid is concerned rests with President Truman.

Most of the delegates are in agreement on the steps to be taken to combat Russia and her eastern European satellite nations.

One of the main problems concerns a suggestion that Germany should be rearmed. The United States' position is that it has no intention of rearming Germany.

Atlantic Pact countries realize that they must coordinate their strategies to keep democratic nations free.

The COLD WAR *Is Fought In Courts Of Law*

Eleven Communist leaders go on trial for conspiracy to overthrow the United States government by force.

Under the stern but impartial eye of Judge Medina they are convicted and sentenced to varying prison terms.

The convicted reds file into a paddy wagon.

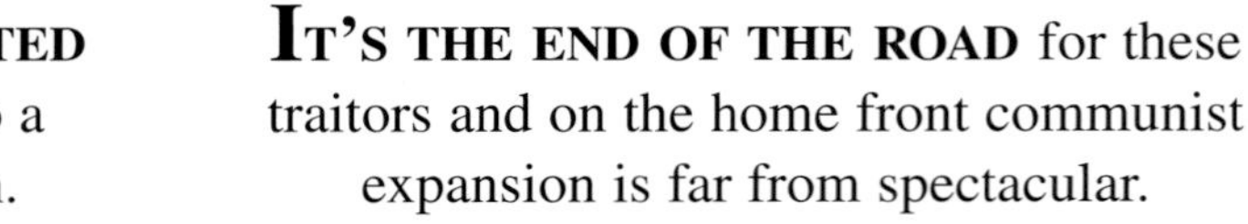

It's the end of the road for these traitors and on the home front communist expansion is far from spectacular.

1949

Harry S. Truman

Inaugurated President Of The U.S. Presents A Four Point Program For Americans To Lead The World In Aiding Poor Countries.

In His State Of The Union Address, President Truman Introduces The Fair Deal Program Which Calls For An End To Discrimination Against Negroes* In Voting Rights And Jobs Making It The First Major Civil Rights Legislation Since Reconstruction.

* Negro was the commonly used term in 1949.

Negroes Invited To Official Inaugural Events In Washington For The First Time.

Truman Declares He Will Use The A-Bomb Again If Necessary.

Federal Housing Aid Banned By Truman Where Religious Or Racial Discrimination Is Practiced.

President Truman Declares That If The U.S.S.R. Does Not Cease Aggression It Will Destroy Itself.

A Housing Bill Allotting Federal Aid For Construction Is Signed By President Truman.

REPORT OF TRUMAN'S ORDER AUTHORIZING BIG A-BOMB EXPANSION LEAKED TO THE PRESS.

President Truman Submits Largest Peacetime Budget In History With The Defense Portion Accounting For More Than One-Third.

Freshman Senator **LBJ**

President Truman Signs Reorganization Act Of 1949.

COMMUNISM

President Truman's Program For Combating The Communist Threat:

- Full Support Of The United Nations;
- Full Support Of The European Recovery Plan;
- A "Collective Defense Arrangement" With Western European Countries;
- Aid In The Industrial Growth Of Underdeveloped Countries By Making Our Scientific Advances Available.

COMMUNISM

ALGER HISS

Perjury Trial Ends In Hung Jury.

Truman Denounces Anti-Communist Hysteria – Ridicules House Un-American Committee's Proposal To Screen Textbooks Used In The U.S. Educational System.

U.S. Communist Leader William Z. Foster Asserts Communist Party Allegiance To U.S.S.R. Should Hostilities Break Out Between The Two Countries.

President Truman Replaces "New Deal" Party Slogan With "Truman Fair Deal."

JUDITH COPLON

Found Guilty Of Stealing U.S. Government Documents For The Soviet Union.

UNITED STATES UNITED STATES

Marshall

DEAN ACHESON Appointed U.S. Secretary Of State On Resignation Of **GEORGE MARSHALL.**

TOM C. CLARK And **SHERMAN MINTON** Appointed To U.S. Supreme Court By President Truman.

The Senate Foreign Relations Committee Publicly Interrogates For The First Time The President's Choice For Secretary Of State.

Controversial Mayor Of Jersey City, New Jersey, Frank Hague, Sees An End To His 32-Year Reign As He Is Defeated At The Polls.

South Carolina Becomes Last State To Legalize Divorce.

President Truman Appoints Georgia Neese Clark Of Kansas Treasurer Of The U.S.

Sam Rayburn Elected Speaker Of The House Of Representatives.

NEW YORK, NEW YORK

After Serving As New York's Liberal Senator For 18 Years, Robert F. Wagner Resigns.

New York's Mayor William O'Dwyer Reelected For Second Term.

Franklin D. Roosevelt, Jr. Wins Seat In House Of Representatives By Huge Majority In Special Elections Held In New York.

Herbert H. Lehman Defeats John Foster Dulles In New York Race For Senate Seat.

Dulles

Louis Johnson Appointed Secretary Of Defense Following James Forrestal's Retirement.

Two U.S. Soldiers Sentenced As Spies In Prague.

A-Bomb And B-36 Called Greatest Forces For Peace By General Carl Spaatz.

B-29 Grounded By U.S. Air Force After Two Crashes In Three Days Resulting In 23 Deaths.

General Omar Bradley Appointed First Chairman Of The Joint Chiefs Of Staff.

DEPARTMENT OF DEFENSE IS CREATED.

U.S. Accuses Eastern Bloc Of Holding Up To 14 Million People In Labor Camps – U.N. Agrees To Investigate.

NORTH ATLANTIC TREATY

Signed In Washington By Belgium, Canada, Denmark, France, Great Britain, Iceland, Italy, Luxembourg, The Netherlands, Norway, Portugal and the United States.

NATO Allies Allotted $5.8 Billion As Truman Signs Arms Aid Bill.

Richard Nixon Among 15 Young Republicans Of The House Of Representatives To Form The Chowder And Marching Society Who Oppose Monthly Bonuses For War Veterans On The Grounds That It Is Too Costly.

EISENHOWER PRESIDENT OF COLUMBIA UNIVERSITY

General Dwight D. Eisenhower Named Temporary Presiding Officer Of Joint Chiefs Of Staff And Chief Military Advisor To President Truman And The Secretary Of Defense.

CIA **The Central Intelligence Act Is Passed By The House Authorizing The Secret Operation Of The Central Intelligence Agency.**

DWIGHT D. EISENHOWER Meets With The Joint Chiefs Of Staff In Key West, Florida To Discuss Domestic And Foreign Cold War Strategies.

GENERAL OMAR BRADLEY is among the high-ranking military leaders to attend this conference.

1949 ADVERTISEMENTS

"Money seemed to evaporate in our family until I started a Christmas Club account —now we save regularly and have bought a new home," writes Mrs. A. M. Lent, Clifton, N. J.

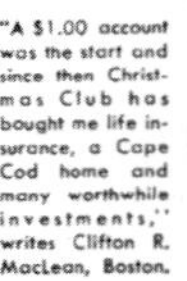

"A $1.00 account was the start and since then Christmas Club has bought me life insurance, a Cape Cod home and many worthwhile investments," writes Clifton R. MacLean, Boston.

"My Christmas Club account enabled my husband and me to satisfy our lifetime dream —a cottage with a little white fence in New Hampshire," writes Mrs. Anna M. Reagan, Dorchester, Mass.

The people pictured here have learned the habit of thrift through Christmas Club.

● These people have saved for a purpose and have sought friendly advice from their banks in developing a systematic savings plan for the future. What they have accomplished is a fine example of the way democracy works.

● You, too, can profit from their experiences in planning for your financial security. But you must act *yourself* . . . you can't depend on others. Join the Christmas Club today at any bank or savings institution displaying this emblem.

JOIN • SAVE
The Christmas Club Way

Christmas Club

a corporation • *Founded by HERBERT F. RAWLL*

341 MADISON AVENUE, NEW YORK 17, N. Y.

"It's the Birdcallers' Convention, and I can't turn this off!"

SIGN OF DEPENDABLE RADIO SERVICE

Is your radio getting out of hand? Is it giving you the bird instead of your favorite station? Don't despair—turn your set over to the serviceman who displays the Sylvania sign. He has accurate Sylvania test equipment to hunt out trouble. He has the skill to put your set in top-notch shape. He'll use those wonderful Sylvania radio tubes to give you better-than-ever reception. No wonder so many people look to the Sylvania sign as the guide to dependable radio service!

SYLVANIA RADIO TUBES
PRODUCT OF SYLVANIA ELECTRIC PRODUCTS INC.

1949

THE ATOMIC

PRESIDENT TRUMAN'S dramatic announcement that Russia has the atom secrets causes state departments all over the world to stir uneasily.

SOVIET REPRESENTATIVE ANDREI VISHINSKY refuses to answer any of the reporter's questions as he enters the United Nations building.

THE GRIM VISION OF AN ATOMIC WAR which would leave complete desolation in its wake is a problem that deeply affects nearly all deliberations of the international forum.

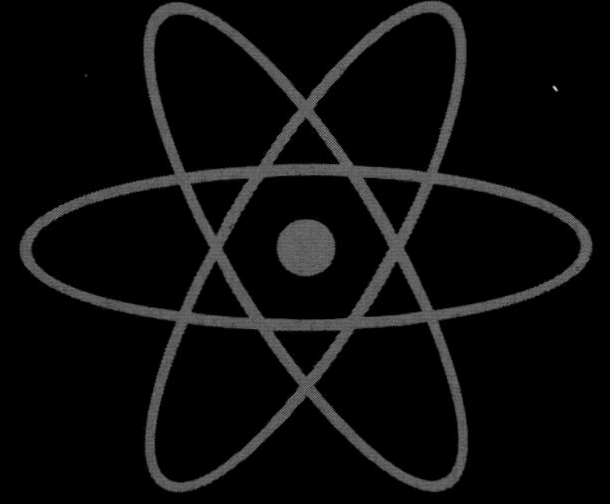

A SYSTEM OF WORLDWIDE atomic control for peace must still be resolved and the United Nations striving toward that end expresses its aim through President Romeo of the assembly:

"The impasse that now exists regarding the international control of atomic energy must be broken and the assembly must face this question squarely for the sake of mankind and for the peace of the world."

The question being asked is will the* ATOM *shatter the world to* FRAGMENTS *or will it be a* BOON *to mankind? Will man* destroy *himself or use his power to make his existence a

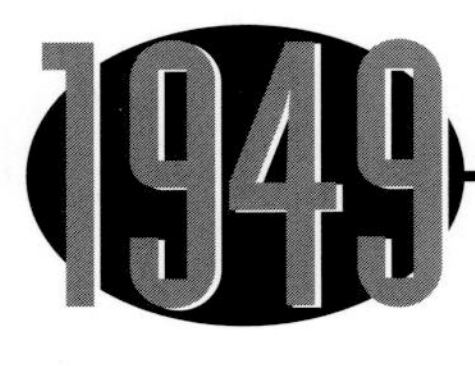

japan

U.S. War Trials In The Far East Come To An End After Convicting 4,200 Japanese Of War Crimes Of Which 720 Were Executed And The Rest Sentenced To Prison.

INDONESIA

In A Ceremony Held In Amsterdam, Queen Juliana Of The Netherlands Transfers Sovereignty Over Indonesia To The Republic Of The United States Of Indonesia.

KOREA

Last Of U.S. Occupying Forces Withdraws From South Korea.

Seoul Government Officially Recognized By U.S.

U.N. Warns Of Danger Of Civil War In Korea.

Only 500 Advisors Remain In Korea As Last Of U.S. Combat Troops Go Home.

LAOS

Proclaims Independence Within French Union.

Vietnam

150,000 French Troops Patrol Border To Prevent Chinese Invasion Of Vietnam.

France Recognizes Independence Of State Of Vietnam.

CAMBODIA

Gets Independence Within French Union.

Siam Officially Becomes Thailand.

In Manila, Rebel Huk Liberation Army Kills Aurora Quezon, Widow Of First Filipino President.

SOUTH AFRICA

South Africa Introduces Apartheid.

Race Riots Erupt In Durban, South Africa Killing Over 100 And Injuring Over 1,000.

RUSSIA

MOLOTOV Replaces VISHINSKY As Soviet Foreign Minister.

Moscow Condemns North Atlantic Treaty Calling It A War Weapon.

In A Secret Test, The Soviets Detonate Their First A-Bomb.

Soviets Block South Korea's U.N. Membership.

Soviet Union Vetoes Nepal's Request For Membership In The United Nations.

Puerto Rico Swears In Former Greenwich Village Writer **Luis Munoz Marin** As First Governor Of Puerto Rico.

Winston Churchill Declares That Threat Of The A-Bomb Is What Kept The U.S.S.R. From Taking Over Europe.

Winston Churchill Is Heckled By Communists During Speech In Brussels Wherein He Calls For European Unity.

1949

Middle East

With Britain Abstaining And Egypt Voting Against, The U.N. Security Council Approves Admission Of Israel By 9-1.

In A General Assembly Vote Of 37-12, Israel Is Admitted As Its 59th Member.

Abba Eban
Is Appointed Israel's First Ambassador To The United Nations.

Britain Grants De Facto Recognition To Israel.

Lifelong Zionist
DR. CHAIM WEIZMANN
Elected First President Of Israel.

With The Support Of His Mapai Party David Ben Gurion Wins Israel's First Parliamentary Elections.

Israel Moves Its Capital From Tel Aviv To Jerusalem.

Israel Celebrates Its First Anniversary As A State.

Prince Rainier III Appointed Ruler Of Monaco On The Death Of His Grandfather, Prince Louis II.

Five RAF Reconnaissance Planes Shot Down By Israeli Fighters.

Four Israeli-Occupied Lebanese Villages Turned Over To Lebanon.

Egyptian Ships Shell Tel Aviv.

Israel And Egypt Agree To Cease Hostilities And Sign An Armistice Agreement On The Island Of Rhodes.

Israel And Syria End 19-Month War As They Sign An Armistice.

U.N. Votes Independence For Libya Effective In 1952.

With 29,000 Communists And 15,000 Royalists Dead A Cease-Fire Is Announced In The Greek Civil War.

Alexander Diomedes Becomes Premier Of Greece.

Israel Adopts Interim Constitution Providing For Parliamentary Form Of Government Similar To Great Britain.

TRANS-JORDAN

Renamed Hashemite Kingdom Of Jordan.

The White House Announces Full Diplomatic Recognition To The Governments Of Israel And Trans-Jordan.

U.N. Mediator Ralph Bunche Negotiates Armistice Agreement Between Trans-Jordan And Israel.

Bunche

THE COUNCIL OF EUROPE

Is Formed By Ten Western European Nations Whose Purpose Is To Prevent A Recurrence Of European Nationalism And To Further Human Rights. Strasbourg Site Of First Meeting.

Britain Recognizes Newly Independent Republic Of Ireland.

Europe Granted $5.43 Billion Aid Under U.S. Foreign Assistance Bill.

Adopts Constitution As Democratic Republic.

Gandhi's Murderer Nathuram Vinayak Is Hanged For His Crime.

CANADA

Newfoundland Becomes Canada's 10th Province.

Under The Leadership Of Louis St. Laurent Canada's Liberal Party Wins 193 Of 262 Seats In The House Of Commons – The Biggest Majority In Canadian History.

Fist Fights Break Out In French Assembly As Communists Try To Defeat The North Atlantic Pact.

Peron ARGENTINA

Amid Growing Opposition Argentina's Juan Peron Declares His Intention To Continue Nationalizing Industry.

Juan Peron Replaces Old Constitution With New One Which Permits Him To Succeed Himself.

YUGOSLAVIA

Yugoslavia's Tito Asks For Economic Assistance From The U.S. To Counter Soviet Blockade. U.S. Grants $20 Million Loan.

Yugoslav War Resistance Leader Laszlo Rajk Admits To Participating In Plot By Tito And The U.S. To Overthrow Hungarian Government.

Russia, Poland And Hungary Terminate Friendship Treaty With Yugoslavia.

U.N. Security Council Admits Yugoslavia.

HUNGARY

Hungary Declared People's Republic.

Budapest Announces Nationalization Of All Foreign And Privately-Owned Industry In Hungary.

Former Leading Hungarian Communist Laszlo Rajk Is Hung For Treason.

Former Interior And Foreign Minister Of Hungary Is Arrested On Charges Of Spying.

German-American Bund Leader Freed In Munich.

Three Million Former Nazis Receive Voting Privileges.

An Estimated 125,000 East Berliners Opt To Live In West Berlin.

No Resolution Is Reached On German Reunification As The Big Four Meetings End In Paris.

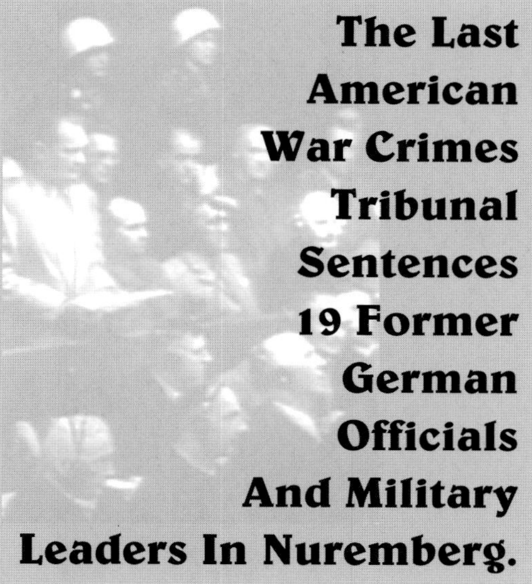

The Last American War Crimes Tribunal Sentences 19 Former German Officials And Military Leaders In Nuremberg.

EAST

The Soviets Create The German Democratic Republic In Response To The New West Germany. Bonn Declares East Germany Illegal.

WEST

Berlin Blockade Officially Lifted.

Berlin Airlift Ends After Completing 277,264 Flights Carrying Over One Million Tons Of Cargo.

Bonn Capital Of Newly Formed German Federal Republic.

Now Eligible For Aid Under The Marshall Plan, West Berlin Mayor Ernst Reuer Asks For Immediate Assistance.

PASSINGS

James V. Forrestal, who recently resigned as the nation's first Secretary of Defense, commits suicide by jumping from a window at Bethesda Naval Hospital. Forrestal, 57, previously served as an assistant to President Franklin D. Roosevelt and was Secretary of the Navy during World War II.

Forrestal

Former Secretary of State **Edward R. Stettinius, Jr.**, the first U.S. delegate to the United Nations and at one time the chairman of the board of United States Steel, dies at age 49.

The Christian Democratic Union Party Wins A Majority Of The Seats In The Lower House Of The New West German Parliament In First Democratic Elections Held In The Country After 1933.

1949 ADVERTISEMENT

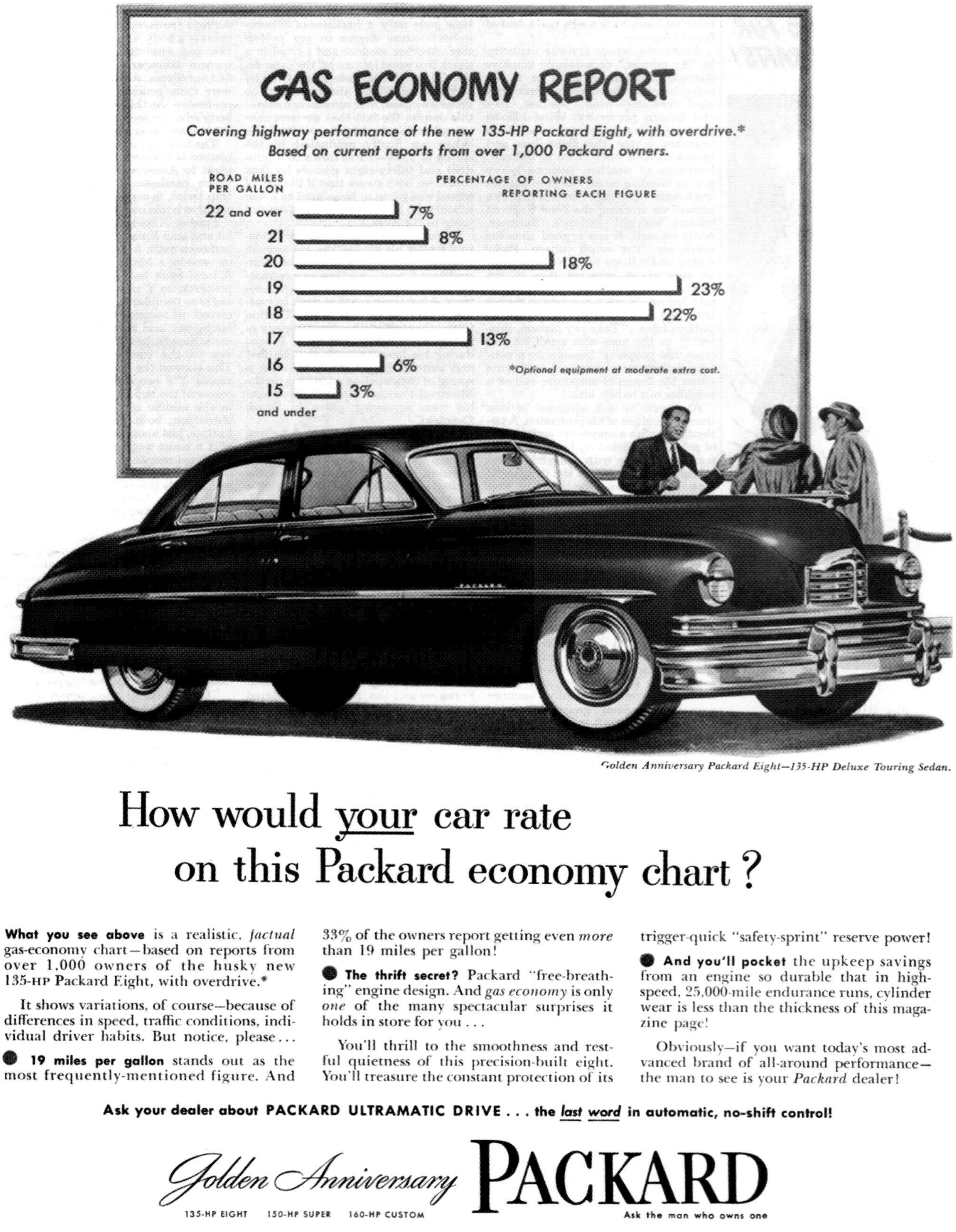
GAS ECONOMY REPORT
Covering highway performance of the new 135-HP Packard Eight, with overdrive.*
Based on current reports from over 1,000 Packard owners.
ROAD MILES PER GALLON
PERCENTAGE OF OWNERS REPORTING EACH FIGURE
22 and over 7%
21 8%
20 18%
19 23%
18 22%
17 13%
16 6%
15 and under 3%
*Optional equipment at moderate extra cost.
Golden Anniversary Packard Eight—135-HP Deluxe Touring Sedan.
How would your car rate on this Packard economy chart?
What you see above is a realistic, factual gas-economy chart—based on reports from over 1,000 owners of the husky new 135-HP Packard Eight, with overdrive.*
It shows variations, of course—because of differences in speed, traffic conditions, individual driver habits. But notice, please...
19 miles per gallon stands out as the most frequently-mentioned figure. And 33% of the owners report getting even more than 19 miles per gallon!
The thrift secret? Packard "free-breathing" engine design. And gas economy is only one of the many spectacular surprises it holds in store for you...
You'll thrill to the smoothness and restful quietness of this precision-built eight. You'll treasure the constant protection of its trigger-quick "safety-sprint" reserve power!
And you'll pocket the upkeep savings from an engine so durable that in high-speed, 25,000-mile endurance runs, cylinder wear is less than the thickness of this magazine page!
Obviously—if you want today's most advanced brand of all-around performance—the man to see is your Packard dealer!
Ask your dealer about PACKARD ULTRAMATIC DRIVE... the last word in automatic, no-shift control!
Golden Anniversary PACKARD
135-HP EIGHT 150-HP SUPER 160-HP CUSTOM
Ask the man who owns one

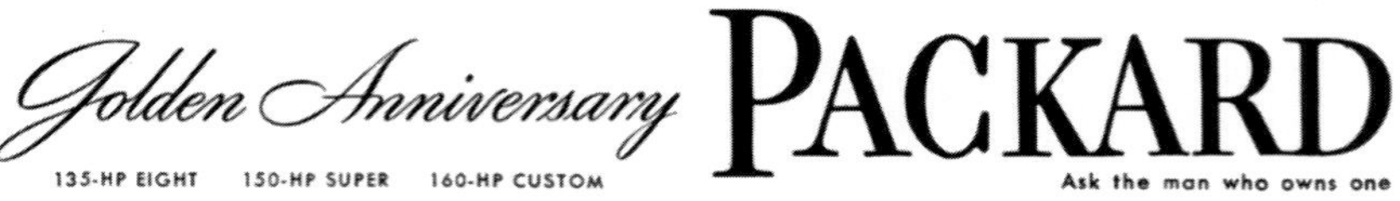

PEOPLE

President Truman Attends Opening Of Photo Exhibition Devoted Exclusively To Him.

The President is pleased with what he sees and points to a picture of him kissing Bess on the cheek.

President Truman gets a particular kick out of the newspaper headline declaring Thomas E. Dewey the winner.

1949

Stars Flock To HOUSTON For Opening Of The Luxurious SHAMROCK HOTEL

Reports Are That The Building Cost Per Room Reaches Record High.

Buddy Rogers *(left)* and **John Barrymore** *(center)* are among the celebrities attending the festivities.

Dorothy Lamour *(left)*, **Andy Devine** *(center)* and **Virginia Grey** *(right)* add more excitement to the occasion.

Pat O'Brien *(left)* and **Ed Wynn** share a laugh.

Funny lady **Joan Davis** clowns around in the lobby.

The cord is cut and the Shamrock is officially open for business.

Arabian Nights 1949

Dominates the theme at the annual ARTISTS AND MODELS BALL Held In New York City

The revelers run the gamut from merely beautiful *(left)* to out of this world *(right)*.

The dancing is a combination of the Fox Trot *(left)* and Lindy Hop *(right)*.

This woman might be called two-faced by some of her friends.

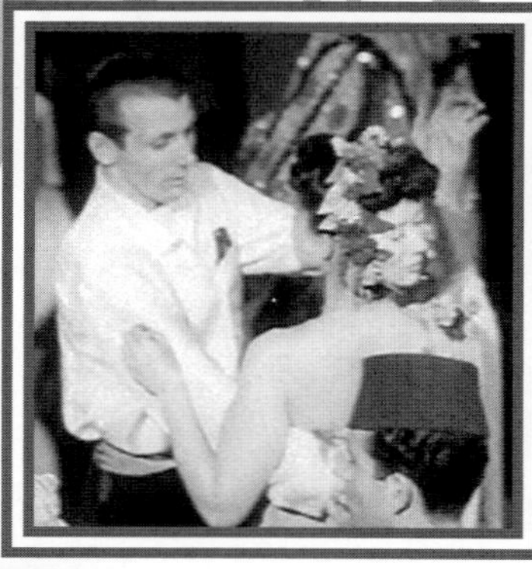

Everything "panned" out just great and a wonderful time was had by all.

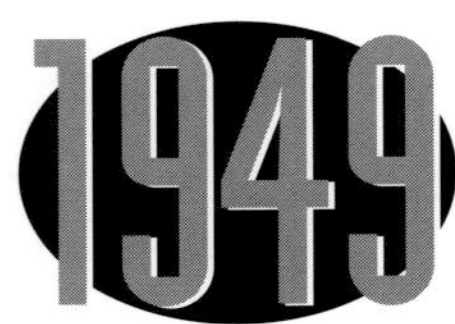

LET 'EM DRINK COKE

The New York State Liquor Authority turns down beer license to Heavyweight Champ Joe Louis and Welterweight Champ Sugar Ray Robinson for their Harlem bar on the grounds some of the other principals are tied to a Chicago mobster.

1949 ADVERTISEMENT

Raggedy Ann & Andy

Each $3.98 *postpaid*

Big, floppy and cuddly, each doll is 18" tall, with bright red mop of unruly yarn hair, tremendous black shoe-button eyes and Raggedy Ann even has an "I Love You" heart just like her storybook counterpart. Their clothing is removable. No. TG2560.

ROBINSON / ROBESON

HELL NO, THEY WON'T GO

In a speech given before the pro-Soviet World Congress of the Partisans of Peace in Paris, U.S. singer PAUL ROBESON states that American Negroes will not fight against the Soviet Union.

PAUL ROBESON returns to the United States after a 4-month tour of eight European countries including the USSR, declaring that the people of the Soviet satellite countries are happy, singing and trying to build for peace.

Brooklyn Dodgers star JACKIE ROBINSON testifies before the House Un-American Activities Committee contradicting Paul Robeson's statement that American Negroes would not fight in a war against the Soviet Union stating that no one has ever questioned his race's loyalty except a few people "who don't amount to much" but that Negroes would stay "stirred up" until Jim Crow disappears in the United States.

JACKIE ROBINSON receives the George Washington Carver Memorial Institute Gold Award for his contribution to the improvement of race relations.

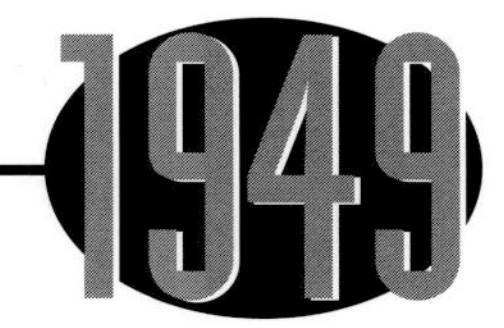

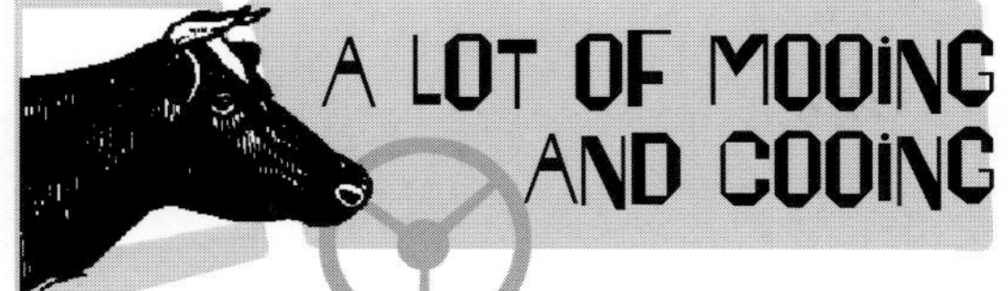

A LOT OF MOOING AND COOING

A disgruntled woman demands her money back after a cow sticks its head in the window of her car while she is watching a movie at a Salt Lake City drive-in.

THIS TICKET'S FOR THE BIRD

William Lasky, son of movie pioneer Jesse Lasky, is fined $100 for driving under the influence of the falcon chained to a glove on his left hand. His excuse: he is rehearsing the falcon for a film.

MAKING A MOUNTAIN OUT OF A MOLE HILL

It's official! Mole Hill, Virginia has changed its name to Mountain.

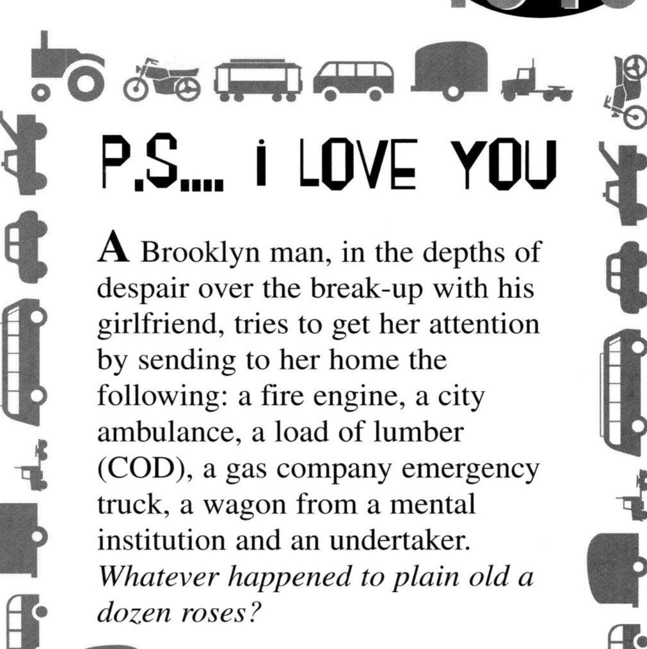

P.S.... I LOVE YOU

A Brooklyn man, in the depths of despair over the break-up with his girlfriend, tries to get her attention by sending to her home the following: a fire engine, a city ambulance, a load of lumber (COD), a gas company emergency truck, a wagon from a mental institution and an undertaker. *Whatever happened to plain old a dozen roses?*

Toga-clad cultist and vegetarian Raymond Duncan arrives in New York to perform his one-man show called "Wobbly-Pop" – the story of the earth's wobbly movement. His philosophy: "Men who grow cabbage and cauliflowers don't start wars."

ANYONE EVER HEAR OF TAKEOUT?

Margaret Truman shocks homemakers by declaring that she hates to cook.

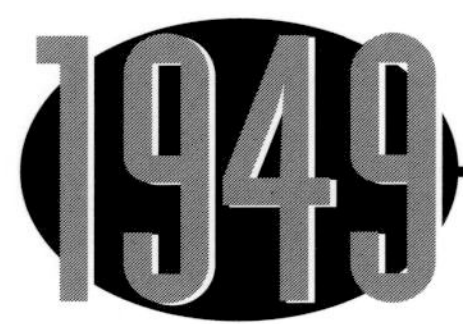

While filming "Annie Get Your Gun," screen star **Betty Hutton** fractures a couple of vertebrae.

Ricardo Montalban is Hollywood's newest romantic lead.

THIS IS NO BIG FOOT

Shoemaker Salvatore Ferragama comes to the defense of **Greta Garbo's** alleged big feet after she orders 70 pairs of shoes in size 7AA stating that her feet are very well-proportioned.

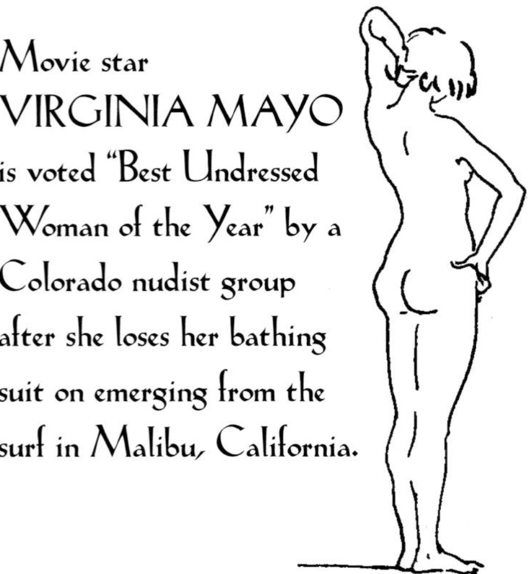

Movie star VIRGINIA MAYO is voted "Best Undressed Woman of the Year" by a Colorado nudist group after she loses her bathing suit on emerging from the surf in Malibu, California.

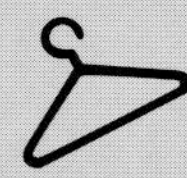

HERE COMES THE BRIDE AGAIN AND AGAIN AND...AGAIN!

Having marched down the aisle three times already, **Joan Crawford** is still selected "The Most Eligible Bachelorette In America" by the American Bachelor Congress. Runner-ups? Anita Colby, Nancy Hawks and Margaret Truman.

Cinema mogul **David O. Selznick** denies rumors of a rift with Jennifer Jones.

On returning to the United States from a tour of Europe, film star **Ella Raines** proclaims American women are the world's sexiest.

Tyrone Power's bride, Linda Christian, plunks down $2,400 for ten Norman Hartnell maternity outfits.

Douglas Fairbanks, Jr. receives an honorary Knight of the Order of the British Empire from King George in recognition of his war services.

Ingrid Bergman complains about the number of Italian photographers interfering with her rehearsals on a film being shot on the island of Stromboli.

Ethel Merman agrees to appear on The Milton Berle Show with the stipulation that she has the stage to herself.

Suffering A Hair Loss

In response to last year's theft of his toupee, former child star Jackie Coogan takes out a $1,000 insurance policy on his new "rug."

LIZZIE & HER MEN

March: ELIZABETH TAYLOR expected to announce her engagement to former West Point football star, Glen Davis.

June: ELIZABETH TAYLOR'S mom announces the engagement of the 17-year old beauty to wartime pilot William D. Pawley, Jr.

ELIZABETH TAYLOR asks if she can keep the $22,000 diamond tiara after she's crowned Princess of the Diamond Jubilee by the Jewelry Industry Council.

Millionaire entertainers **Bob Hope** and **Bing Crosby** strike oil in west Texas oilfields making them millionaires once again.

Bob Hope voted #1 funny man in America with **Milton Berle** and **Jack Benny** running closely behind.

Jack Benny to pay $1,030,000 in taxes for his share of the $2,260,000 sale of his program to the Columbia Broadcasting System.

GUESS WHO'S COMING TO DINNER

The Friar's Club, exclusive bastion of the rich and famous men of Hollywood, breaks with tradition and invites a woman to dinner by the name of **Sophie Tucker**, honoring her 43 years in show business.

11-year old film star **Natalie Wood** chosen "Child of the Year" in first nationwide observance of Children's Day.

Helen Hayes, whose daughter died of polio, is named chairman of the National Foundation for Infantile Paralysis.

Hollywood mogul 47-year old DARRYL F. ZANUCK signs 20-year contract making him 20th Century Fox production boss for 10 years and advisor for the next 10 at an annual salary of $260,000.

Ailing from pleurisy, Hollywood film star **Ann Sheridan** collapses on the set of "I Was A Male War Bride."

Ray Bolger's nose gets broken in a playful exchange with Sugar Ray Robinson who aimed for Bolger's hat but connected with his nose instead.

Lady Astor denounces Hollywood's preoccupation with sex adding that educated women are far more important to the world.

Fed up with eight years of posing scantily clad **Ava Gardner** announces that she is through with "cheesecake."

Movie director **Nicole Vedres** shoots film in Paris starring Pablo Picasso, Jean-Paul Sartre, Andre Gide, Jacques Prevert and Frederic Joliot-Curie.

France faces its third big robbery in two days when four armed men hold up the Aga Khan and his wife, the Begum, and get away with an estimated $785,000 in jewels. The couple was en route from Cannes to Deauville to visit their honeymooning son, Prince Aly, and his new wife, American screen star **Rita Hayworth.**

Aly Khan announces that his beautiful wife, Princess Margarita A.K.A. **Rita Hayworth**, is expecting a baby.

SOMEONE UP THERE IS LISTENING

On trial in Nuremberg for being a major Nazi offender, Friedrich Geyer exclaimed: "May I drop dead if that charge is true." And so he did, having a stroke in the courtroom.

- Former Secretary of State GENERAL GEORGE C. MARSHALL is appointed president of the American Red Cross by President Truman.

- Republican SENATOR MARGARET CHASE SMITH denies any plans for running for the presidency.

- DR. RALPH J. BUNCHE named Father of the Year by National Father's Day Committee but declines post as Assistant Secretary of State for the Middle East and Africa.

- In a **LOOK** Magazine poll, 100 Washington correspondents vote ROBERT A. TAFT the senator who contributes the most to the country's welfare.

- J. EDGAR HOOVER celebrates his 25th anniversary as head of the FBI.

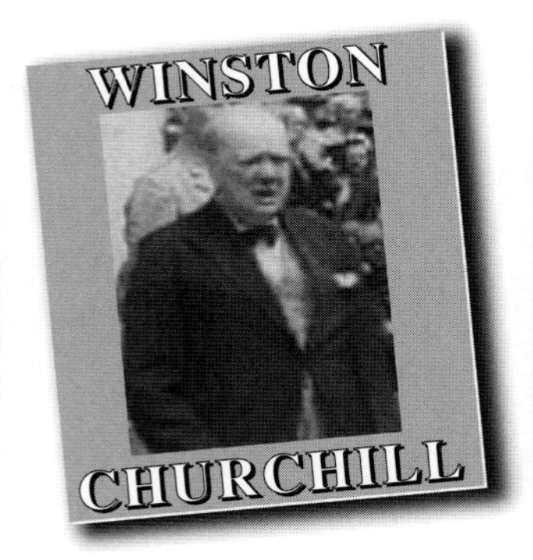

Chosen MAN OF THE HALF-CENTURY By TIME Magazine

- Indian PRIME MINISTER NEHRU visits the United States for the first time.

- 77-year old JUDGE LEARNED HAND celebrates his 40th anniversary on the bench to which he was originally appointed by President Taft in 1909.

- The Women's National Press Club nominates Portland, Oregon's MAYOR DOROTHY MCCULLOUGH LEE outstanding American Woman in government.

- JOSEPH CARDINAL MINDSZENTY, found guilty of treason and sentenced to life imprisonment, petitions the U.S. Minister in Budapest asking him for help in escaping Hungary.

- Head of International Longshoreman's and Warehouseman's Union, HARRY BRIDGES, indicted on charges of perjury and conspiracy for denying he was a communist in his naturalization proceeding.

- WILLIAM H. HASTIE becomes first Negro sworn in as judge of the United States Circuit Court of Appeals.

PASSINGS

An important figure in the Alcoholics Anonymous organization, **Anne Smith** dies at age 68.

Former Brigadier General **Prince Louis II**, ruler of Monaco since 1922 and one of Europe's wealthiest men, dies at 78, leaving his kingdom to grandson Prince Rainier.

The U.N. General Assembly stops its business for seven minutes to pay tribute to MRS. ELEANOR ROOSEVELT on the occasion of her 65th birthday.

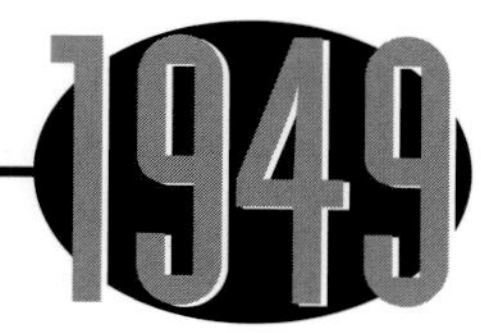

Bess Truman

MRS. HARRY TRUMAN dazzles 300 guests at a reception for Mrs. Perle Mesta, newly appointed minister to Luxembourg and Mrs. Georgia Neese Clark, new Treasurer of the United States, when she shows up 20 pounds lighter. The secret? She eliminated salt from her diet.

PRESIDENT & MRS. TRUMAN celebrate their 30th wedding anniversary.

Super war hero turned actor/writer AUDIE MURPHY announces his 8-month marriage to Wanda Hendrix is in trouble.

The youngest GI to receive the Congressional Medal of Honor, PFC. JAMES HENDRIX, survives 1,000 foot plunge to the ground after his two parachutes fail to open during a practice drop over Fort Benning, Georgia.

Miss America 1948 Bebe Shopp denounces falsies as being dishonest.

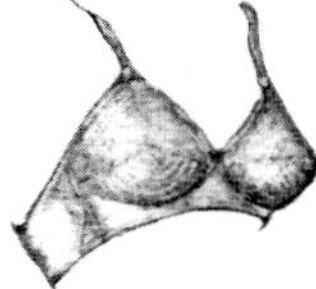

Jacque Mercer of Littlefield, Arizona is crowned Miss America 1949.

LOWELL THOMAS suffers injuries in a horse accident in the Himalayas.

SONG SUNG BLUE, EVERYBODY KNOWS ONE... OR TWO

Obviously upset at the announcement of her impending divorce from Elliott Roosevelt, FAYE EMERSON quietly weeps at Edith Piaf's opening night performance when she finds herself seated across from her soon-to-be-ex during a particularly sentimental love song.

In his AUTOBIOGRAPHY **Albert Einstein** sums up his OPINION OF EDUCATION with the following thought:

"It is, in fact, nothing short of a miracle that the modern methods of instruction have not yet entirely strangled the holy curiosity of inquiry."

The **Harvard Hasty Pudding Club** chooses **MARGARET TRUMAN** as WOMAN OF THE YEAR.

TOMMY MANVILLE offers $5,000 reward to anyone who can prove his phones are tapped.

BATTLE OF THE BULGE

PRESIDENT TRUMAN is waging a battle with his weight trying to get his current 176 pounds down to his doctor's recommendation of 170.

The Harvard graduate school of business administration receives pledge of $5,000,000 from philanthropist JOHN D. ROCKEFELLER if it receives matching funds towards its $20,000,000 goal.

Cardinal Spellman accuses **Eleanor Roosevelt** of being a bigot due to her stand on the separation of Church and State issue.

At a dinner held at New York's Waldorf-Astoria Hotel, MILTON BERLE receives Interfaith in Action's Award for furthering the cause of racial understanding.

Comedian DANNY KAYE, tennis stars Louise Brough and Mrs. Margaret Osborne du Pont and former High Commissioner of the Philippines Paul V. McNutt among passengers aboard a Pan American Airways airliner bound for New York from Ireland when one of the four engines catches fire forcing the plane to return to Shannon airport.

More than 100,000 Israelis line the cortege route as the remains of the Father of Zionism, Dr. Theodor Herzl, are brought back from Vienna to a final resting place on the highest hill in Jerusalem.

NOBEL PEACE PRIZE

Lord John Boyd-Orr of Brechin, Great Britain

WINSTON CHURCHILL is the man with the most ***Sex Appeal*** according to actress BETTY HUTTON.

WINSTON CHURCHILL–who turns 75–on the subject of age quips: ***"I am ready to meet my Maker. Whether my Maker is prepared for the great ordeal of meeting me is another matter."***

Billie Holiday

The Lady Really Has the Blues

On being acquitted of a possession of opium charge, blues singer Billie Holiday laments over the disappearance of her manager, John Levy, adding that—despite all—she would still take him back if he returns.

- In Paris world-famous diva, **Mary Gordon**, proclaims that American opera is dying and that there are no more great singers. Remedy? Send American singers to Europe to train.

- Composer **Richard Strauss** celebrates his 85th birthday.

- **Margaret Truman** to resume her musical career.

- President Truman in attendance at the Women's National Press Club as 88-year old **Gandma Moses** receives annual award for art.

- On turning 93, playwright **George Bernard Shaw** is relieved that he has reached his second childhood.

BLONDIE creator Chic Young receives Best Cartoonist choice from the National Cartoonists' Society.

ARTHUR MURRAY STUDIOS NAMES BEST NON-PROFESSIONAL DANCERS

General Mark W. Clark
Bing Crosby
Joe DiMaggio
Doris Duke
N.Y. Mayor William O'Dwyer
Esther Williams

The Artists League of America Picks The Most Perfect Features

Cheekbones:	**Jane Russell**
Ears:	**Margaret Truman**
Eyes:	**Princess Margaret**
Legs:	**Linda Darnell**
Forehead:	**Duchess of Windsor**
Thighs:	**Esther Williams**
Lips:	**Rita Hayworth**
Nose:	**Madame Chiang Kai-shek**

LONDON BRITCHES

The London Master Tailors' Benevolent Association chooses PRINCE PHILIP, 27, as the perfect example of proper dressing for all occasions.

American contralto MARIAN ANDERSON happily gets her voice back after the successful removal of a cyst on her throat.

1949 ADVERTISEMENT

Shop Refreshed . . . Have a Coke

When you shop, you pause—first at one shelf, then another. Make one stop *the pause that refreshes* with an ice-cold bottle of Coca-Cola . . . and shop refreshed.

Make another stop where you see handy six-bottle cartons on display, and take some with you. It's the way to be refreshed at home.

DRINK Coca-Cola

DRINK Coca-Cola

Shop Refreshed

5¢

"GOOD" COP, "BAD" ACTOR

Currently playing the part of a hero policeman in his new film "The Big Steal," **Robert Mitchum's** role switches as he's sentenced to 60 days in prison for possession of marijuana.

Given a week to get his affairs in order before serving his 12-18 month sentence for the vehicular homicide killing of "Gone With The Wind" author, Margaret Mitchell, HUGH GRAVITT is in another collision with a truck.

What could very well be the unproduced murder weapon in that infamous murder trial, LIZZIE BORDEN'S ax is discovered in a hidden wall in the chimney of her house.

TOKYO ROSE (Iva D'Aquino) is found guilty of making treasonable broadcasts over Radio Tokyo and sentenced to ten years in prison and a $10,000 fine.

A "CRUMMY" ENDING

Gangster PHILIP "Little Farfel"* COHEN'S career comes to an abrupt end when his body is found murdered gangland style on a remote road near Valley Stream, New York.

*(*Yiddish for "little crumb")*

NO, I WON'T CHANGE MY WICKED WAYS

Mobster MICKEY COHEN denies ever having a meeting with Dr. William Graham about a conversion.

Hollywood's No. 1 racketeer MICKEY COHEN, his companion Dee David and a bodyguard are shot as they leave Sherry's Restaurant on the Sunset Strip.

Reputed head of a nationwide $2 billion slot machine racket, FRANK COSTELLO, denies being boss of New York and bribing public officials adding that he didn't even have the connections to get a traffic ticket fixed.

THE PRINCE GETS SHORN

Heir to the British Crown, 9-month old Prince Charles, takes his first haircut without shedding a tear and says "ta-ta" to the Royal Barber who leaves the Young Prince with some curls.

Prince Charles celebrates his first birthday weighing in at a royal 25 pounds, six teeth and a vocabulary consisting of Pa-Pa and Mum-Mum.

Shah of Iran, Mohammed Reza Pahlavi, is injured in assassination attempt.

Britain's King George VI observes his 54th birthday with a quiet family gathering and a 41-gun salute.

Princess Elizabeth flies to Malta to visit her husband, the Duke of Edinburgh, and celebrates their second wedding anniversary with champagne and a three-tiered cake.

POP GOES THE MEASLES

Baby Prince Charles can't see his Mum for a few days as she's recovering from a case of the measles.

GETTING HER KICKS

Princess Margaret shocks the guests at an American Embassy party in London by appearing in a Cancan chorus line wearing the traditional lace panties and long black stockings.

HIE THEE TO A TAILOR

Princess Margaret's sister, Princess Elizabeth, disapproves of the plunging neckline on Margaret's new Dior gown and takes immediate steps to have the offending neckline lifted.

MARLENE DIETRICH violates protocol by smoking at a Royal Dinner before the King is toasted.

PRINCESS MARGARET stuns guests at a charity ball by lighting up a cigarette, causing a startled Briton to sniff that with cigarettes costing $.49 a pack, only a Princess could afford to smoke.

Glamorous Movie Star Rita Hayworth and Heir to one of the World's Most Fabulous Fortunes Prince Aly Khan Marry on the French Riviera

The Prince and his new bride stand on the steps of the church and greet well-wishers.

Crowds gather to catch a glimpse of this beautiful couple.

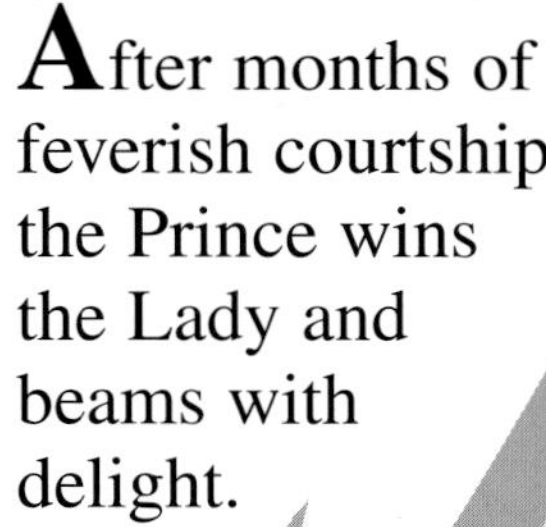

After months of feverish courtship the Prince wins the Lady and beams with delight.

Vice President Alben Barkley ties the knot with the former Mrs. Carleton S. Hadley

Mr. Barkley is the first vice president to marry while in office and in these troubled times happy endings are a delight.

1949 Coupling

UNCOUPLING

Jackie Cooper & June Horne Cooper

Dean Martin & Betty MacDonald

Nancy Walker & Garry Moore

Joe Louis & Marva Trotter Barrow Louis

Prince & Princess Aly Khan

Burgess Meredith & Paulette Goddard

Shirley Temple & John Agar

Franklin Delano Roosevelt, jr. & Ethel du Pont Roosevelt

Errol Flynn & Nora Eddington Flynn

Joanne Dru & Dick Haymes

Margaret Whiting & Hubbell Robinson, jr.

Deanna Durbin & Felix Jackson

Ginger Rogers & Jack Briggs

Governor Adlai Stevenson & Ellen Borden Stevenson

Marie Wilson & Alan Nixon

Merle Oberon & Lucien Ballard

Ingrid Bergman & Dr. Peter Lindstrom

TWICE IS NOT ENOUGH

Errol Flynn Announces His Engagement To 20-Year Old Rumanian Princess Irene Ghica, Making This Next Trip Down The Aisle #3.

1949 ADVERTISEMENT

EVER HAPPEN TO YOU?

After being a popular Joe in your neighborhood did you ever find yourself left out of little parties all too often? Maybe you wondered if there was some kind of a hex on you? Well, Chum, there probably was! A guy can get careless every now and then, and the news* gets around pretty fast. The welcome mat won't be out again until you get over your trouble.

You wangled an introduction to a swell girl and invited her out on a super-special date. Along about ten she began to act indifferent, and pleaded to be taken home. A headache, (she said). The whole evening shot . . . to say nothing of a few bucks. Were you burned up! It probably never occurred to you that you, yourself, were the "headache." And for this* reason.

Were you last to be let in after waiting for hours to see the Big Wheel? Under your breath you probably called the Big Wheel a lot of choice names. Maybe he had a good reason for stalling. After all, it's only human nature to put off disagreeable things as long as possible. And, Brother, when you've got it* you sure can be disagreeable!

On a moonlight night did you ever try for a kiss from your steady Sweetie Pie and have her haul off and bat you in the kisser? Why? Why? Why?? You just didn't get it. Perhaps you were "that way"* (It can happen to anyone) . . . and when you are, they'll do it every time.

Did you ever go after a job that you knew was right down your alley, only to lose it to another fellow with no better qualifications than yours? You probably wondered what the hair-line decision was that threw the job the other fellow's way. Well . . . very often it's as delicate a matter as this*.

*** How about you?** If you ever have come face to face with a case of halitosis (unpleasant breath) you know how it repels you. You don't have to guess what kind of a reception you'd meet if you, yourself, were guilty. So, why risk offending? Why take chances on makeshift remedies when there's a delightful and *extra-careful* precaution against simple bad breath? Use Listerine Antiseptic, the standby of millions. You merely rinse the mouth with it . . . especially before any date, and, lo! your breath becomes sweeter, fresher, less likely to offend. Stays that way, too. Not for seconds. Not for minutes. But for hours usually. When you want to be at your best never, never omit Listerine Antiseptic.

*Listerine Antiseptic halts the fermentation of food particles in the mouth, a cause of so much bad breath not of systemic origin. Lambert Pharmacal Co.

LISTERINE ANTISEPTIC

the Extra-careful Precaution against Offending

THE MEN WHO RULE THE WORLD

(ACCORDING TO THE OVERSEAS PRESS CLUB)

Dean Acheson (USA)
Clement Attlee (Britain)
Joseph Stalin (USSR)
Harry Truman (USA)
Walter Reuther (USA)
Winston Churchill (Britain)
Jacques Duclos (France)
Marshal Tito (Yugoslavia)
Mao Tse-tung (China)
Jawaharlal Nehru (India)
Jan Christian Smuts (S. Africa)
Pope Pius XII
King Abdullah (Jordan)
Nikolai Bulganin (USSR)
Vyacheslav Molotov (USSR)
Paul Hoffman (USA)
Douglas MacArthur (USA)
Ernest Bevin (Britain)
Charles de Gaulle (France)
Francisco Franco (Spain)
Paul Henri Spaak (Belgium)
Chaim Weizmann (Israel)
Juan Peron (Argentina)

ADDITIONAL MOVERS AND SHAKERS

(ACCORDING TO NEW YORK POST REPORTER MAX LERNER)

Albert Einstein (Scientist)
Arnold Toynbee (Historian)
Carl Gustav Jung (Psychiatrist)
Bernard Shaw (Writer)
Andre Gide (Writer)
William Faulkner (Writer)
Albert Schweitzer (Theologian)
Jacques Maritain (Theologian)
Sir Alexander Fleming (Discovered Penicillin)
Eleanor Roosevelt (Moral Symbol Of The Western Democratic Creed)
John Dewey (Philosopher)
Bertrand Russell (Philosopher)
Pablo Picasso (Artist)
T.S. Eliot (Writer)
Jean Paul Sartre (Writer-Philosopher)
Martin Buber (Theologian)
Reinhold Niebuhr (Theologian)

Albert Einstein and Thomas Mann

Thomas Mann receives the Goethe Prize from the City of Frankfurt on his first visit to Germany since his self-imposed exile in 1933.

RCA chairman, Brig. General David Sarnoff, receives United Nations citation for his support of the United Nations and contribution to human rights.

Charles A. Lindbergh receives the Wright Brothers Memorial Trophy for significant public service.

The 1949 Freedom Award is shared by David E. Lilienthal, Atomic Energy Commission chairman, and General Lucius D. Clay.

1949 ADVERTISEMENT

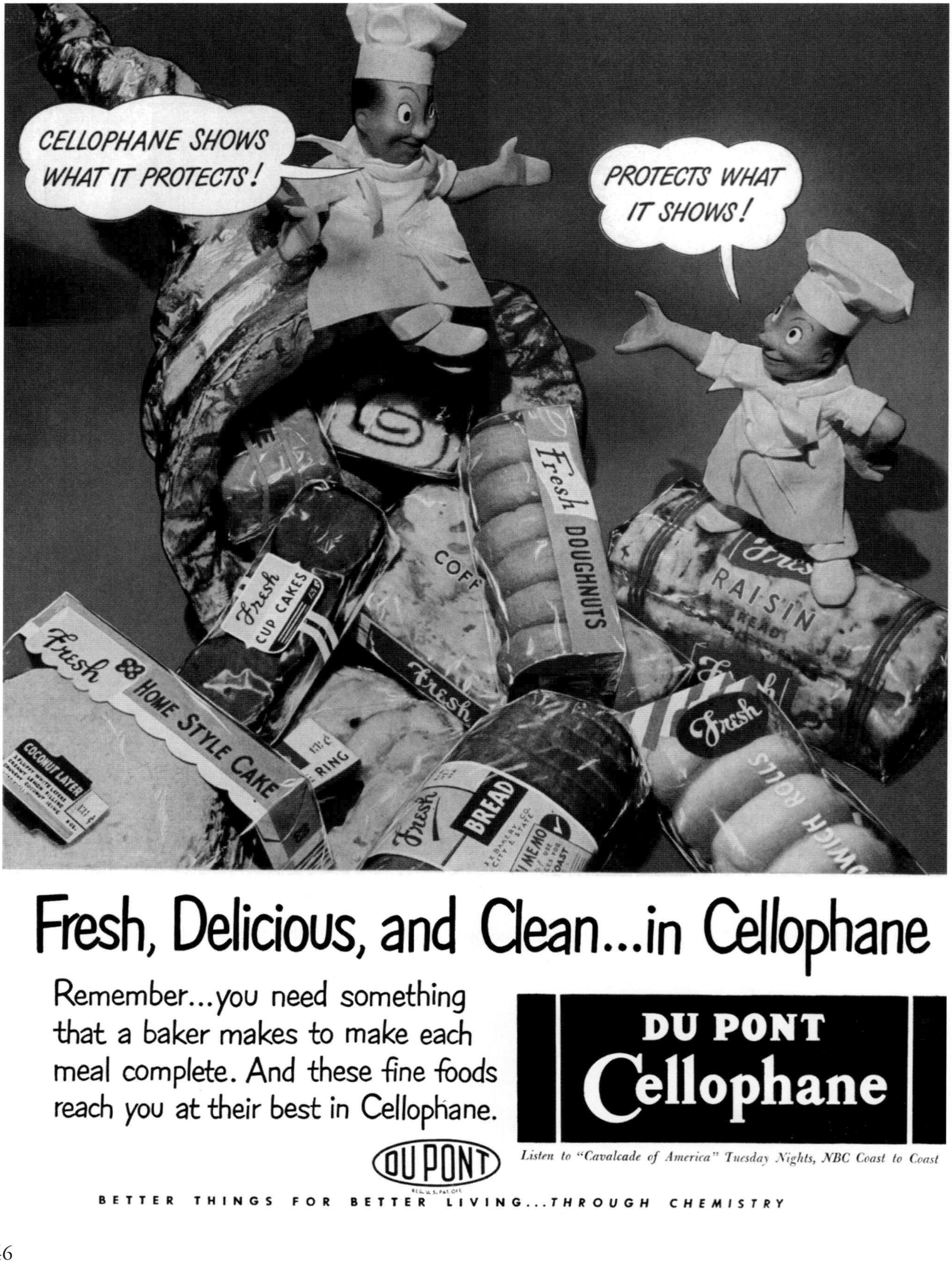

CELLOPHANE SHOWS WHAT IT PROTECTS!

PROTECTS WHAT IT SHOWS!

Fresh, Delicious, and Clean...in Cellophane

Remember...you need something that a baker makes to make each meal complete. And these fine foods reach you at their best in Cellophane.

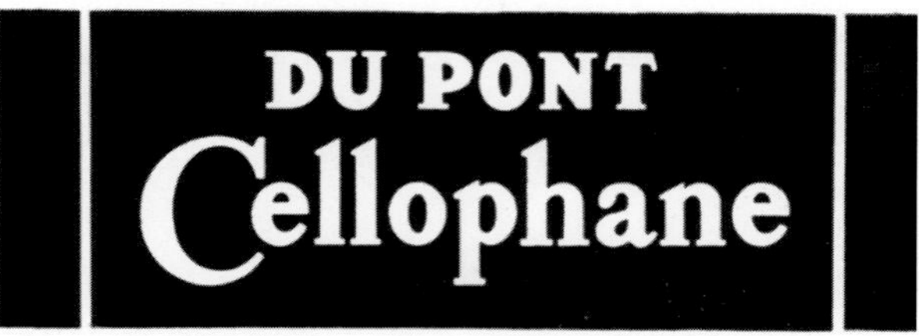

Listen to "Cavalcade of America" Tuesday Nights, NBC Coast to Coast

DU PONT

REG. U.S. PAT. OFF.

BETTER THINGS FOR BETTER LIVING...*THROUGH CHEMISTRY*

Human Interest

KATHY FISCUS

The nation's attention is riveted on the fate of 3-year old Kathy Fiscus who falls into an abandoned artesian well in San Bernardino, California.

Rescue attempts begin to try to save little Kathy who fell in the well while playing with her sister and friends.

Crowds gather in vigil and to offer their prayers.

Friends of Kathy wait quietly hoping she will be saved.

Every engineering resource is enlisted (above) including pumping air to the little girl (right) whose faint cries could be heard for a short time.

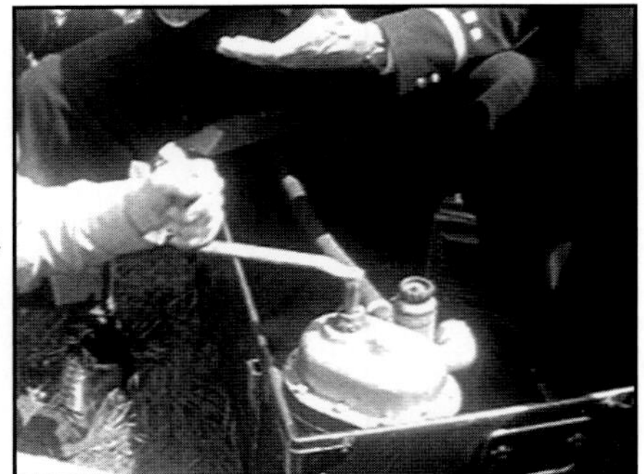

Rescue workers risk their lives in a frantic attempt to save the child.

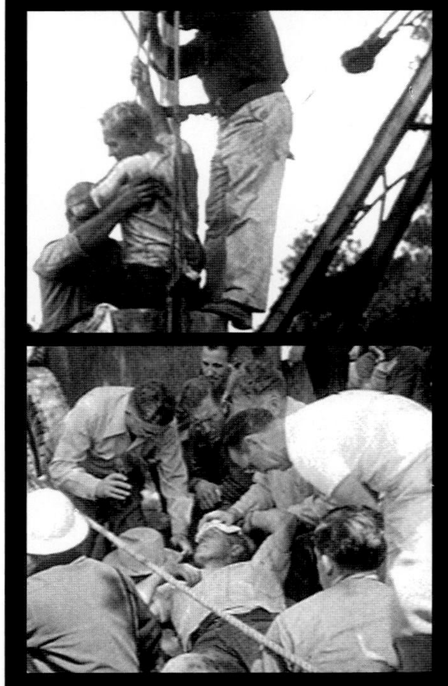

This courageous man worked until he was overcome with exhaustion.

In the grim race that continued into a second night, seeping water had to be pumped out.

Despite the continuing prayers of family and friends who gathered in support, the outcome is tragic for after 50 hours of a valiant effort, Kathy is found dead – a victim of suffocation shortly after she fell into the well.

netless in chicago

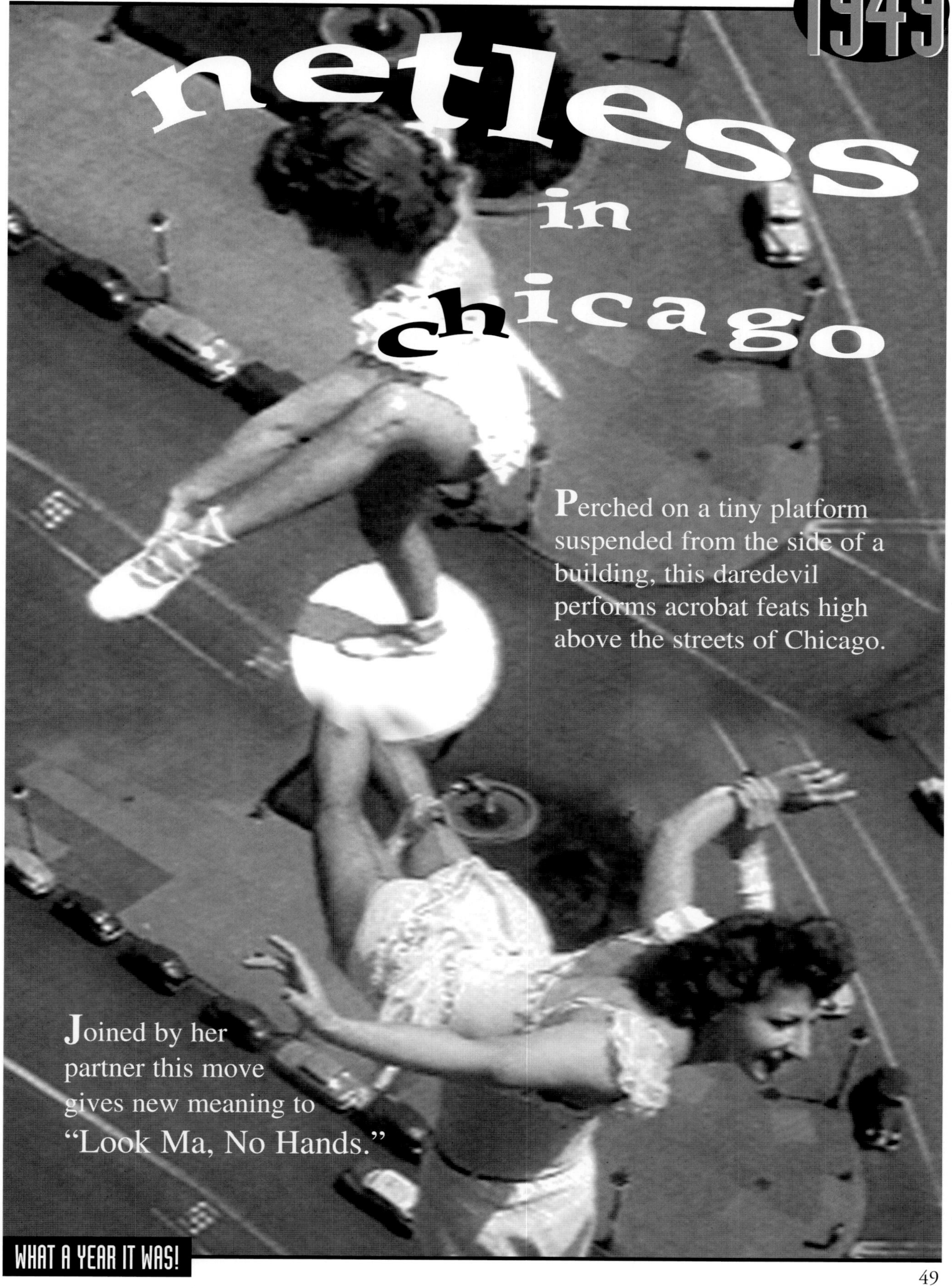

Perched on a tiny platform suspended from the side of a building, this daredevil performs acrobat feats high above the streets of Chicago.

Joined by her partner this move gives new meaning to "Look Ma, No Hands."

1949 the Tall and The Short Of It!

The big fella used to be with the circus, but has now settled down in Portland, Oregon where he dodges doorways and tries not to stand out in a crowd.

The headline news is: **Thompson Is 8′7″ Tall And Weighs 460 Pounds.**

Tallest man in the world, Clifford Johnson, gets his size 22E shoes shined.

RENOVATIONS BEGIN ON THE WHITE HOUSE.

THE BUTLER DID IT!

Rudyard Kipling's daughter, Mrs. Elsie Bambridge, sues her butler in Cambridge, England on the grounds that he was nipping away at her vintage wine collection and replacing the missing wine with a variety of liquids, including water, tea and ink.

THE U.S. SUPREME COURT

...Upholds Trenton, N.J. Ordinance Banning "Loud And Raucous" Sound Trucks On The City Streets.

...Rules That A Nevada Divorce Could Be Declared Invalid If The Divorced Party Is Not Personally Served In Nevada.

...Reaffirms The Constitutionality Of The Housing And Rent Act Of 1949.

A LONG WALK TO BORROW A CUP OF SUGAR

With fewer than two people per square mile, Nevada is the most sparsely populated state of the union.

NATIONAL FREEDOM DAY

Is Established By A Presidential Proclamation.

THERE'S GOLD IN THEM THAR HILLS

The Gold Rush Which Began With The Discovery Of Gold At Sutter's Mill, California Celebrates Its 100th Anniversary.

WHAT DO YOU MEAN I SAID "I DO?"

According To A Leading Attorney, It's Not A Good Idea To Make A Contract With Someone Who Is Drunk As He Can Void The Contract When He Sobers Up.

ARE YOU NOW OR HAVE YOU EVER BEEN...?

University Of California At Berkeley Now Requires Non-Communist Oaths To Be Taken Both By Faculty And Administrative Employees.

National Education Association Votes To Bar Members Of The Communist Party From Teaching.

With Two Of Ten Hollywood Screenwriters Refusing To Answer Questions Regarding Alleged Communist Party Affiliations, The District Of Columbia Rules That Freedom Of Speech Does Not Include The Right Of A Witness To Maintain Silence In Hearings Before Legislative Committees.

The Supreme Court Accepts For Direct Ruling A Case Involving Discrimination In Public Services On Southern Railroads.

Negro Workers Can Sue Railroads And Railroad Unions For Alleged Discrimination In Employment Practices According To New Supreme Court Ruling.

Theophilus Roberts Is The First Student To Enroll In The Langston University Law School For Negroes And Ends The Year With Above-Average Marks At Which Time The School Closes Since Mr. Roberts Is The Only Student In The School.

Jay Saunders Redding Is Appointed First Negro Professor At Brown University.

22-Year Old Wesley A. Brown Is The First Negro To Graduate From The U.S. Naval Academy In Annapolis.

CLIFF HILL A Young Negro Arrested For A Disturbance In A Negro Roadhouse Is Taken From A Jail Cell In Irwinton, Georgia And Is Beaten And Shot To Death Making Him The First Lynching Of The Year.

WHAT'S A GUY TO WEAR?

When asked why the Ku Klux Klan wore disguises, Grand Dragon Dr. Samuel J. Green responded it is because "so many people are prejudiced against the Klan."

The Governor Of Alabama Signs Bill Making It Illegal To Wear Hoods Or Masks In Public.

WHO GETS THE SHEET CONCESSION?

Estimated Membership In The Newly Formed Knights Of The Ku Klux Klans Of America Is 265,000 Nationwide.

Michigan's Saginaw-Chippewas And Wisconsin's Stockbridge-Munsees Become First American Indian Tribes To Gain Full Self Rule.

Six Of The Sixteen Surviving **Civil War Veterans** Meet In Indianapolis For The 83rd And Last Encampment Of The Grand Army Of The Republic.

Evangelical Minister Billy Graham

350,000 People, Including Gene Autry And Jane Russell, Show Up To Hear 31-Year Old Billy Graham Speak Under A Ringling Brothers Circus Tent Kicking Off A Post-War Revival Of Religion In America. Graham Is Offered A Screen Test By Cecil B. DeMille.

laughter...

YOU ARE HOW YOU LAUGH
(A Classification)

SOUND:	THE TRAITS:
A-A	Cheerful & Kind
E-E	Egotistic & Moody
I-I	Children & Old People
O-O	Melancholy & Pessimistic
U-U	Hypocrite & Cheat

A New Religious Sect Based On Laughter Is Founded In Japan Requiring That You Live Right By Being Able To Laugh At Anything Or Nothing.

PRAISE THE LORD AND PASS THE SURFBOARDS

Most Worshippers Remain In Their Cars At The 8:30 A.M. Services Conducted In North Hollywood, California By Rev. Norman L. Hammer Giving The Parishioners An Early Start On Their Sunday Outings.

Pope Pius XII Calls For Internationalization Of Holy Sites In Palestine Including Jerusalem.

LET 'EM DRINK TEA

The Mormon Church's Salt Lake City Desert News removes 85,000 offensive comic strips from its Sunday comics supplement showing Ernie Bushmiller's "Fritzi Ritz" character Phil warming a coffee cup with his oversized pipe.

AND THE CHILD SHALL MARRY THEM

Four-Year Old Rev. Marjoe Gortner, An Ordained Minister In The Old Time Faith, Inc. In Los Angeles, Creates Quite A Clerical Stir After He Performs A Marriage Ceremony.

The Pope Excommunicates Everyone Involved In The Trial And Treason Conviction Of Hungary's Cardinal Mindszenty.

The Vatican Excommunicates Roman Catholics Who Are Communist Party Members Or Sympathizers.

In its first revision in sixty years, a new U.S. Catholic catechism states that there is no salvation outside the Church.

To Correct The Shortage Of Clergy, The Bishop Of Prague Ordains Its First Two Women Priests In The Czechoslovak Catholic Church.

1949

President Truman Appoints 5-Year Old Richard Feeney, Son Of A White House Aid, To Head Feeding Of The Squirrels Residing On The White House Lawns After Richard Complains That The Squirrels In Lafayette Square Are Fatter.

THE READER IS LEFT HOLDING THE RAG

The Chicago Sunday Tribune Runs The Costliest Ad In History - A Page Made Of A New Rayon Material Called "Miracloth" Which Evaporates The Printing When Dipped In Water, Turning The Page Into A Cleaning Cloth.

AIN'T THAT THE CAT'S

Illinois Governor Adlai E. Stevenson Vetoes A Bill Requiring Cats To Be Leashed.

baby-boomers

The Baby Boom Registers 3.58 Million Births.

The First Baby-Boom Children Are Ready To Toddle Off To Kindergarten With Educators Predicting A 39% Increase In School Attendance.

The Population Of The United States Reaches A Record Of 148,527,000.

Lauren Bacall And Humphrey Bogart Have Their First Child – Stephen.

The New York Regency Club Skyrockets The Game Canasta Into National Popularity.

comics

Chic Young's Comic Strip **"Blondie"** One Of The Most Popular In The World.

Walt Kelly's **"POGO"** Makes Its Newspaper Debut And Becomes The First Nationally Syndicated Comic Strip.

Former Hobo, Clyde Lamb, Kicks Off His **"HERMAN"** Comic Strip In The New York World-Telegram.

The Seattle Times Drops The **"Li'l Abner"** Comic Strip On The Grounds Of It Being Distasteful Because The Hillbilly Hero Believes He's Eaten One His Parents.

The Famous Savoy Hotel In London Is Accused Of Cheating Its Customers By Serving Under-Measured Booze Using Inferior Brands.

Nazi Field Marshall Erich Von Mannstein, Last German To Be Tried By The Allies For War Crimes, Is Found Guilty On Nine Of Seventeen Charges And Receives 18-Year Prison Sentence.

NOW LET'S SEE, WHAT IS A COW ON A TRIANGLE AGAIN?

A new sign language for motorists has been proposed by traffic specialists of the Economic Commission For Europe which would substitute pictures for lettered signs creating a worldwide common language such as:

SIGN OF A COW:	Cattle Crossing
CAR CAREENING ON TWO WHEELS:	Slippery When Wet
SMOKING LOCOMOTIVE:	Railroad Crossing
CHILDREN'S FIGURES:	School Or Playground

FOR THE FIRST TIME IN ITS HISTORY, ENGLAND GRANTS RANK OF KING'S COUNSEL TO TWO WOMEN.

IN YOUR EASTER BONNET WITH ALL THE CHOCOLATE EGGS UPON IT

For the first time in nine years, the French are looking forward to chocolate Easter eggs as rationing is lifted on butter, milk, cheese and chocolate.

RUSSIA BANS STUDY OF THE ENGLISH LANGUAGE ON THE GROUNDS IT IS A DECADENT SUBJECT.

HOW SWEET IT IS

After Seven Years Of Candy Rationing In England, "Lollipop Week" Kicks Off Treating British Kids To The Sweetest Of The Sweets Which Disappear Off Store Shelves In Record Time.

1949 Divorce, American Style

A Bridgeport, Connecticut Judge Grants Mrs. Catherine Tichnor A Divorce On The Grounds That Her Husband Hit Her In The Face With The Family Cat.

NUMBER OF MARRIED COUPLES: 35,323,000

TOP 10 COMPLAINTS BY UNHAPPY WIVES

1. Lack Of Communication
2. Impatience
3. Overly Critical
4. Lack Of Affection
5. Business Dominates His Thoughts
6. Quick To Anger
7. Nervous Or Emotional
8. Complains Too Much
9. Poor Sex Drive
10. Only Thinks Of Himself

HOWEVER, The Average Wife Is Healthier Than Her Husband, Will Live Several Years Longer Than Him And Her Layer Of Insulating Fat Makes It Easier For Her To Adjust To Temperature Changes.

39 STRIKES AND YOU'RE OUT!

And in Los Angeles, poor Mr. Oldfield wins a divorce on the grounds his wife would never let him go to a baseball game or even listen to a game on the radio during their 39 years of marriage. The judge's advice? "Go to a game every day and yell at the umpire. It will do your ego good."

THE BRITISH SEX REPORT
– THEY CAN TAKE IT OR LEAVE IT – BUT MOSTLY LEAVE IT

1. **Perfectly Happy Without Sex: 31%**
2. **Sex Is Wrong: 26%**
3. **Sex Could Prove Harmful: 56%**
4. **Sexual Relations Are Unpleasant: ..54%**
5. **Sex Is Important To Happiness: ...33%**

...SEWING

Surpasses Cooking As The Favorite Domestic Science High School Course For Girls.

WHY MARRIED WOMEN WORK:

1 Financial Necessity;
2 To Buy Luxury Items;
3 Prefer Working To Housework Routine;
4 A Minority Are Exceptionally Talented Who Have Careers From Sheer Interest;
5 A Hedge Against The Future;
6 An Outlet When The Children Leave Home;
7 Emotional And Financial Resource If Marriage Ends.

Wives Are Employed And One-Third Of All Employed Women Are Married And Living With Their Husbands.

New York University Begins Its 60th Year Of Teaching The Only Women's Law Course In The Country.

A "Ladies Only" Dance Hall Opens In Osaka Where Male Dance Hosts Have To Be Well-Bred, Well Brought Up, Handsome Gentlemen With Previous Employment Recommendations.

According To Etiquette Experts, A Lady Need Not Remove Her Glove To Shake Hands Although Men Are Still Expected To Give A Gloveless Handshake.

Roses And Daisies Are The Flowers Of Choice On The First Anniversary Of The Day Honoring All Never-Been-Married Women Over 35.

BRINGING HOME THE BACON, TOO

More Than 16,000,000 American Women Hold Payroll Jobs Accounting For 27% Of The Work Force.

WHAT 1,000 CHICAGO WORKING GIRLS WANT

1. A Husband
2. A Typewriter
3. A Pressure Cooker

AVERAGE WORK WEEK: 42.2 HOURS

TEEN SPEAK
The Popular Phrase:
"How low, (or smart, or stupid, or corny, or frantic) can you get?"

Teenagers List Dancing As One Of The Top Three Date Activities And Sock Hops Originate When Dancers Remove Their Shoes In Order To Protect Gym Floors.

I WANNA DANCE, PLEASE ASK ME

Friday Night Is The Big Dance Night As Teenagers Gather In Church Basements, School Gyms, Y's, Teen Canteens And Settlement Houses To Dance To Their Favorite Big Band Records.

Boys: Don't cut in on the same girl twice in a row.

Girls: Don't dance with another girl as the boys don't like to cut in.

SCHOOL DAYS

Students At New York's Hunter College Model School For Exceptional Children Participate In An Experimental Project Where The Students Learn Typing At A Faster Rate Than Most Adults And Find Typing Helpful In Improving Their Spelling Skills.

Between 30-50 Adults Out Of 100 In America Are Either Studying Or Planning To Study At The End Of Their Work Day.

England Builds Its First Prefabricated Aluminum Schoolhouse And Manufacturers Erect One At Neuilly, France In 30 Hours.

TO NECK OR NOT TO NECK, THAT IS THE QUESTION (A POLL)

Concerning Whether Or Not It's OK To Neck Or Pet On A Date, 90% Of The Boys Said "Yes" While Only 74% Of The Girls Said "Yes."

DAD, CAN I BORROW THE CAR?

16-Year Olds Can Now Get A Junior License Under A New New York State Law.

THE LITERACY SCORES

Denmark	99.5%
Germany	99.5%
Great Britain	99.5%
The Netherlands	99.5%
Norway	99.5%
Sweden	99.5%
Switzerland	99.5%
United States	97.3%
Underdeveloped Countries	20%

Much To The Chagrin Of Greenwich Village Residents, Wrecking Crews Begin Demolition Of A Block Of 120-Year Old Homes On Washington Square South To Make Way For A New Law Building For The Country's Largest School, New York University, With An Enrollment Of 47,000 Students.

THE FIRST CAMPUS OF THE NEW YORK STATE UNIVERSITY SYSTEM IS ESTABLISHED.

The Samuel H. Kress Foundation Donates $8,000,000 For The Development Of The New York University-Bellevue Medical Center.

New York City's Wall Street Becomes One-Way, East And A Bit Downhill.

Hey Buddy, You Wanna Fix A Bridge?

Plans Are Completed For The Reconstruction Of The Famous Old Brooklyn Bridge.

A BRIDGE TOO FAR

The Proposed Liberty Bridge Which Is To Span The Narrows At The Entrance To New York Harbor Between Brooklyn And Staten Island With An Historic Length Of 4,720 Ft. Receives Official Authorization.

NEW YORK, NEW YORK, WHAT A WONDERFUL TOWN

- 40 Buildings 36 Stories High Or Higher.
- The World's Busiest Corner Is 34th & Broadway.
- 716,065 Buildings And 5,000 Miles Of Streets.
- Enough Trees To Shade The Entire Population Of The City – That's Three People To Each Tree.

THE PLANE TRUTH

NEW MEANING TO FLYING BY THE SEAT OF HIS PANTS.

Lt. J.L. Fruin Becomes First American Pilot To Use His Ejection Seat And Is Brought Safely To The Ground.

Air Travel Is Getting Very Popular.

Regularly Scheduled Freight Flights Begin As Four U.S. Charter Services Receive The Green Light To Compete With Mail-Passenger Planes.

The First Woman Pilot To Fly Around The World, Britain's Flying Housewife, Mrs. Richard Morrow-Tait, Says She Wanted To Show What An Ordinary Housewife Can Do Besides Changing Diapers And Pushing Baby Carriages.

"The Lucky Lady" An Air Force B-50 Bomber, Makes First Nonstop Around-The-World Flight In 94 Hours, 1 Minute Using Inflight Refuelling And Fuel Conservation Through The Use Of Cruise Control.

Crispin Vergo Becomes The First Person Convicted Of Planting A Bomb On An Airplane In Order To Collect Life Insurance.

A British Overseas Airway Jet Airliner Is First To Fly From London To Tripoli In A Record 6 Hours, 38 Minutes At 100 M.P.H., Faster Than The Fastest Propeller Airplane.

THEY'RE GETTING UP AND STAYING UP!

Airline Safety At Record High With Only 1.0 Fatality Rate – The Lowest In History.

The U.S. Air Force Becomes Fully Independent Of The Army.

World War II Veteran Howard B. Unruh Goes On Shooting Spree In Camden, New Jersey Killing 13 People.

40-Year Old GEORGE N. CRAIG Becomes First Veteran Of World War II To Be Elected To National Commander Of The American Legion.

"ENOLA GAY,"

The B-29 Superfortress That Dropped The First Atomic Bomb On Hiroshima, Takes Its Place In History In The Smithsonian National Air Museum.

Having Entertained Millions Of Servicemen During The War,

THE USO

Opens A State Headquarters In Syracuse As A First Step In A Fund-Raising Campaign.

WILLIAM P. ODOM Is Killed In The National Air Races In Cleveland, Ohio After Setting A New Round-The-World Record Of 397.071 M.P.H. Odom had earlier broken the long-distance nonstop record for light planes, flying 5,300 miles from Honolulu to New Jersey.

RECORD TEMPERATURES

New York Sees A Record High Of 78.6 Degrees In July – The Hottest It's Been In 78 Years.

A Record Freezing Spell Hits Southern California With Temperatures Plummeting to 14 Degrees Destroying One-Fifth Of The State's Citrus Fruit Crop.

For The First Time In The History Of Local Weather Bureaus, A Heavy Snowfall Blankets Southern California Including Los Angeles, Pasadena, San Diego And Palm Springs.

The Atlantic City Pier Sustains $250,000 In Fire Damages.

FIRE, FIRE

The Metropolitan Opera House Suffers $10,000 In Fire Damages.

GENERAL MOTORS

Holds Its First New Car Show In Nine Years.

DO YOU SMELL SOMETHING FUNNY?

A water shortage hits New York necessitating the natives to go without bathing and shaving on designated days as well as abstaining from watering sidewalks and washing cars.

1949

War Correspondent Ernie Pyle Is Reburied On Oahu, Hawaii, At The New National Memorial Cemetery Of The Pacific.

Crippling Strike Of London Dock Workers Causes King George VI To Declare State Of Emergency.

The French Luxury Liner ***"Ile de France"*** *Docks In New York After Her First Post-War Crossing.*

When The Lights Go On Again...

After 10 Years Of Dark Streets, Store Fronts And Neon Signs, The Lights Go On Again In London Sparking A Return To London's Pre-Wartime Gaiety – Restaurants And Night Clubs Now Open Until 2:00 A.M.

A New Version Of The Chain Letter, The Get-Rich-Quick Pyramid Clubs Sweep America.

A CORNY DISCOVERY

Two Young Harvard Scientists Discover Corn Cobs Dating Back To 2,000 B.C. In A New Mexico Cave.

A Search For Noah's Ark Led By A U.S. Expedition Ends Unsuccessfully After 12 Days On Turkey's Mount Ararat.

HOT TOYS:

Plastic Erector Sets, Toni Permanent Wave Dolls And Schmoos.

FIRE DOG TO THE RESCUE

Mooch, A Dalmatian Pooch, Receives The Paddy Reilly Medal From The Greenwich Village Humane League For His Heroic Actions In Rescuing A Dog From A Fiery Death On Christmas Eve.

New Bloom for Your Garden

GLOIRE DE GUILAN: 2-1/2 to 4 Inches Across Clear Pink Double Flowers With a Strong Fragrance And Grow On Three To Five Foot Bushes.

WHITE DAWN: A Large Double Blossom White Climbing Plant With A Gentle Fragrance.

FASHION: A Double Flower Of Coral And Peach Pink, These Moderately Fragrant Plants Grow Two To Three Feet Tall.

MAKE MINE SONOMA

California Wineries Are Trading In Foreign Names Such As Burgundy And Chablis And Are Now Featuring Their Own County Or District Of Origin On The Labels. So Look For Such Names As Sonoma, Napa Or Livermore Valley Along With The Name Of The Grape. And To All You Gourmets Out There ... How Nice That You Are No Longer Ashamed To Order Domestic Wines In Other Than A Whisper.

giving them a new twist

Pretzel Experts Gather In Philadelphia To Discuss The Decline In The Old-Time Twister Citing The Lack Of Emphasis On Training Which Is Being Geared More And More To Mechanical Rather Than Traditional.

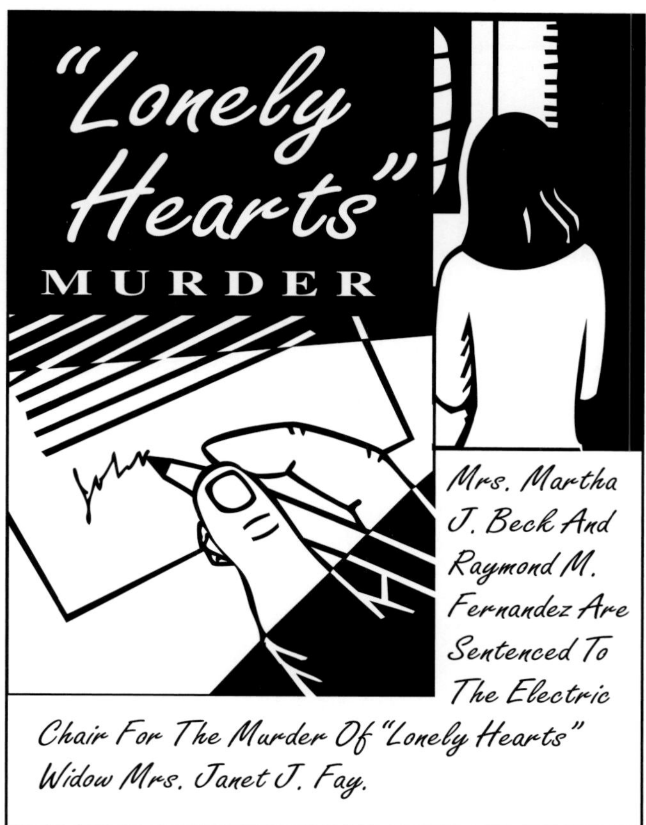

Mrs. Martha J. Beck And Raymond M. Fernandez Are Sentenced To The Electric Chair For The Murder Of "Lonely Hearts" Widow Mrs. Janet J. Fay.

240,000 Bars Of Soap Are Shipped Out Of Philadelphia To European Children – A Gift From American Children Living Along The Eastern Seaboard.

Normandy, France Exports Delicious Camembert Cheese For The First Time Since Before The War.

The U.N. General Assembly Holds Meeting At The Site Of Its New Permanent Home As Cornerstone Is Laid.

WE SIMPLY CANNOT MAKE UP OUR MINDS

The 29th International Congress Of The World Union Of Freethinkers Split Over The Issue Of Cooperation With Extreme Left-Wingers.

California Governor Earl Warren Signs THE KATHY FISCUS BILL Tightening Restrictions Against Abandoned Excavations And Wells To Prevent Similar Tragedies Like The Death Of 3-Year Old Kathy.

The Fifth Attempt To Repeal Oklahoma's 42-Year Old Prohibition Law Goes Down In Defeat.

HE TOOK THE MONEY AND RAN

After Looting The Bank's Vault Of $884,000 In Cash And Securities, Richard H. Crowe, Assistant Manager Of A National City Bank Branch, Disappears.

A NOT SO SWEET ENDING

The "Chocolate Soda Gang," Who Fortify Themselves With Chocolate Sodas Before They Commit Robberies, Are Captured In New York As A Result Of A Telephone Tip To The Police.

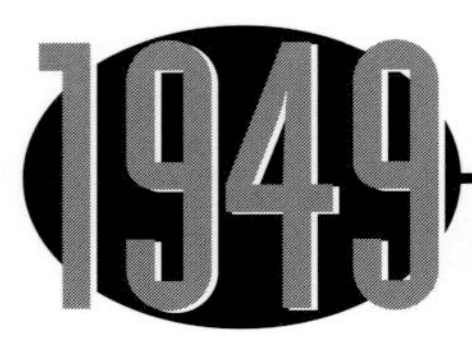

THE MAN WITH THE LONGEST NAME IN THE WORLD *or* HOW DID YOU SAY YOU SPELL YOUR NAME?

Mr. Diwan Bahadur Sir Tiruvalyangudi Vijayaraghavacharya.

His Friends Call Him Diwan. His Children Call Him Pop. The Ladies Call Him "Dear One."

MISS PIGGY No 311,

Survivor Of The First Atomic Blast At Bikini, Leaves Her Pen At The Naval Medical Research Center In Bethesda, Maryland And Heads For Her New Home In The Zoo Weighing In At 600 Pounds –

Up From The 50 Pounds She Weighed At The Time Of The Blast.

EMPLOYMENT

	TOTAL # IN LABOR FORCE	# EMPLOYED
MALE	43,988,000	41,426,000
FEMALE:	18,588,000	17,575,000

BUBBLE, BUBBLE, TOIL & TROUBLE

Parents complain to the police that the children of Southfield Township, Michigan seem to have an inordinate supply of bubble gum. The police discover 100 large cartons of the chewy substance had been left at the town dump, thereby accounting for the pockets and mouths full of gum.

Romance Magazines

Top The List Of Best-Selling Magazines.

SALT ANYONE?

Pepper Prices Rise Due To The Scarcity In The World Markets.

The Average Long Distance Call Is Connected In About One-And-One-Half Minutes.

Housewives Across America Stock Up As A Coffee Shortage Sweeps The Country Causing The Price To Skyrocket From $.27 A Pound To $.46.

Sentimental Journey

As their way of saying "Merci Beaucoup" for the Friendship Train sent to France last year, the French send the United States a Gratitude Train consisting of 49 boxcars – one for each state including the District of Columbia which arrives in New York aboard the freighter "Magellan" to a rousing reception.

1949 ADVERTISEMENT

1. By the age of twelve, the average boy and girl are mature enough to recognize the value of precious time, to plan the days more methodically and thoughtfully, and to handle a precision instrument with care. When you buy a watch, ask your jeweler: "Does it have a quality Swiss jeweled-lever movement?" If it does, this feature is your best assurance of accuracy, dependability, and value. See the newest in watches during "The Watch Parade," Oct. 24—Nov. 7.

2. Practical watches to give young, active people are water-repellent and shock-resistant. These features, like the self-winding watch, calendar watch, chronograph, and chronometer, are Swiss developments. In every watch, *it's the movement that counts—be sure your watch has a quality Swiss jeweled-lever movement.*

How old should a youngster be before he gets his first good watch?

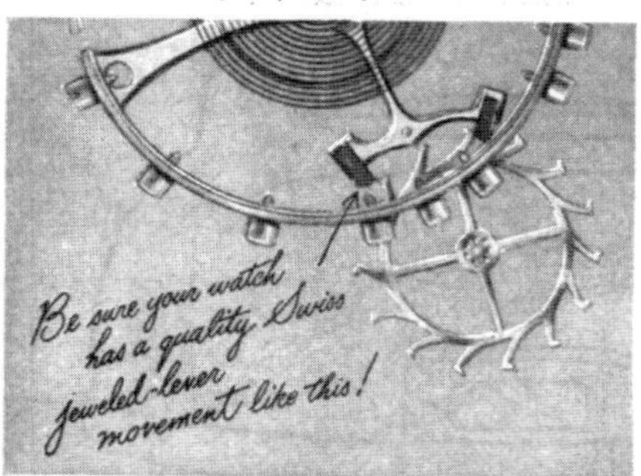

3. To get the most for your money, choose a watch with a quality Swiss jeweled-lever movement. For the jeweled-lever is the mechanical "heart" that keeps your watch running accurately with a minimum of wear. *Don't be fooled by so-called "watch bargains"—you usually get just about what you pay for.*

4. Swiss craftsmen were the first to use jewels in watch movements—in 1704. Today, the quality Swiss jeweled-lever movement stands for timekeeping excellence the world over. That's why *a smart Swiss watch is a treasure of lasting pride—for you—or for the fortunate one who receives it from you.*

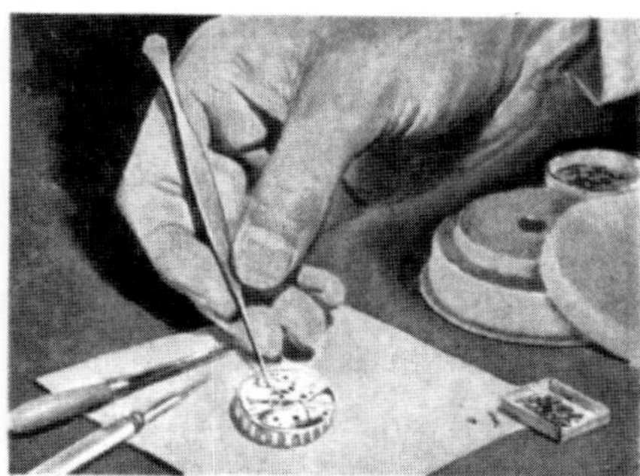

5. With the aid of the Swiss Watch Repair Parts Program, your jeweler can service quality Swiss watches economically and promptly. For watches are your jeweler's business. So, *when you buy a new watch, rely on a jeweler in whom you have confidence—he'll show you the best jeweled-lever Swiss movements in your price range.*

For the gifts you'll give with pride—let your jeweler be your guide

The WATCHMAKERS OF SWITZERLAND

NEW WORDS &

ACTH
Adrenocorticotrophic hormone, produced by pituitary gland, potential arthritis cure.

CELLANO
A kind of human blood.

CHUCKS
A teenage term for anything comical.

AIRDENT UNIT
A tool for drilling teeth using compressed air.

COMMUNITY COLLEGE
A junior college in local communities where students can attend classes while still living at home.

CORTISONE
A hormone from the adrenal cortex, experimentally used on arthritis sufferers.

AUTOMATION
An automatically operated system or process.

AVIONICS
Electronics used in the aeronautic field.

COUNCIL OF EUROPE
An organization of democratic European countries.

BANTHINE
An oral drug for peptic ulcers.

BEEFCAKE
To expose men's well-built torsos. Similar to the feminine "cheesecake."

DIXIEGOP
Dixiecrats & Republicans opposed to many of President Truman's policies, chiefly civil rights.

BINAC
An electronic machine that uses binary numbers for calculations.

BOLD NEW PROGRAM
President Truman's Fair Deal program, especially Point Four.

DOLLAR GAP
The financial situation when there is an imbalance of imported and exported items.

BOTOGENIN
Matter discovered in the Mexican yam, possible cortisone source.

BRUSHED LEATHER
Suede.

DRAMAMINE
A drug used to prevent motion sickness.

EXPRESSIONS

ECONOMY HOUSE
A little home.

FAIR DEAL
The new program introduced by President Truman in his State of the Union speech.

ME-TOOISM
Republicans that comply with Democrat methods.

FIREBIRD
Common name of the XAAM-A-1 rocket-driven bomb.

FIVE PERCENTER
A businessman that charges 5 percent for services, especially for obtaining government contracts for clients.

NO-DAY (WORK) WEEK
Work stoppage, strike euphemism.

FREEZE-DRYING
A way to preserve food for future use by freezing then drying with heat.

PARAMILITARY
Equivalent in significance to traditional military.

HAYLIFT
An air lift operation that drops bales of feed to starving cattle during severe storms.

PARLAY
To profit victoriously.

POINT FOUR
The point in President Truman's Fair Deal plan that stresses assistance to under-developed countries.

PHYTOTRON
A Cal Tech lab where the effects of weather on plant life is studied.

JETLINER
A jet-propelled airplane.

KIGMY
An Al Capp devised cartoon animal.

KILLER SHIP
A ship used to find and destroy adversarial submarines.

PRESTRESSED
Concrete strengthened with high-tension steel wires.

PYRAMID (FRIENDSHIP) CLUB
A get-rich-quick plan.

NEW WORDS & EXPRESSIONS

RADIAC SET
A small device that detects radioactivity.

ROTOCHUTE
A supersonic parachute for research equipment.

SANITY CODE
The National Collegiate Athletic Association's code to control the selection and financial support of athletes.

SPACE MEDICINE
A potential branch of medicine to study the effects of outer space on the human body.

TEENICIDE
Reckless teenage driving.

TITOISM
Marshall Tito of Yugoslavia's communist-based convictions.

UNESCAN
U.N.E.S.C.O. participant.

UNI
The united military command of the Council of Europe.

UNIAIR
The air command division of the Council of Europe.

UNIFORCE
The air, sea and land command of the Council of Europe.

UNILION
Commander chairman of all military divisions of the Council of Europe.

UNITER
Land command of the Council of Europe

UNIMER
The sea command of the Council of Europe.

VEEP
Endearing term for the vice-president of the United States.

VEEPA, VEEPESS
Endearing term for the wife of the vice-president of the United States.

BUSINESS

Biggest Dividend In History Paid By General Motors Amounting To $190,000,000.

A Compromise Lease Agreement Which The Governor Helps Mediate Is Reached Between Five Major Airlines And The New York International Airport At Idlewild, Queens Ending A Two-Year Dispute.

With The Purchase Of A Two-Engine Convair Airliner, American Airlines Becomes The First Major Airline In The World To Own A Completely New, Post-War Fleet Of Aircraft.

General George C. Marshall Is Elected To Board Of Directors Of Pan American Airways.

Charles H. Percy, 29, Is Elected President Of Bell & Howell Co., Making Him One Of The Youngest Chief Executives Of A Major Company.

Celebrating The History-Making Opening Of A $7,000,000 Nabisco Plant In Houston, Senator Tom Connally Assures Baking Company Officials That There Won't Be Any Communists In Texas.

Conrad Hilton Announces He Purchased A Controlling Interest In New York's Elegant Waldorf-Astoria.

The Bank Of Manhattan Celebrates Its 150th Anniversary.

A Group Of Southern California Postal Workers Found Fedco, A Unique Member-Only Discount Retail Chain.

1949 UNION NEWS

In a memorial to miners killed or injured in 1948 and to protest the appointment of James Boyd as director of Federal Bureau of Mines, John L. Lewis orders 425,000 United Mine Workers east of the Mississippi to begin 2-week work stoppage.

500,000 STEEL WORKERS QUIT AS STRIKE BEGINS IN PITTSBURGH

62,000 STRIKE AT FORD MOTOR PLANT IN DETROIT

ENDING THE 42-DAY STRIKE, U.S. STEEL SIGNS TWO-YEAR UNION CONTRACT.

John L. Lewis' bid for U.M.W. reaffiliation is rejected by A.F.L.

The right of states to ban the closed shop is upheld by the U.S. Supreme Court.

Trolley, bus, subway and elevated workers accept a small wage increase ending their 10-day strike in Philadelphia.

Train service comes to a screeching halt on the Missouri Pacific lines as 5,200 employees go on strike.

It's a 40 hour week without pay reduction starting next fall for the nation's 1,000,000 non-operating railroad workers.

Accusing Ford Motor Co. of speeding up the assembly lines, workers at two plants pull walk out.

Against left-wing opposition, Walter Reuther is re-elected international president of the United Automobile Workers.

Labeled a communist-dominated union, United Electric, Radio and Machine Workers of America are expelled from the C.I.O.

National Labor Relations Board Rules That Peaceful Picketing In Support Of A Secondary Boycott Is A Violation Of Taft-Hartly Act.

According to the Supreme Court, states are not prohibited from imposing more severe restrictions on labor union security contracts as this action does not violate the Wagner Act or Taft-Hartly Act.

800 U.S. steel companies receive demand from United Steelworkers of America for fourth wage increase.

Failing to reach agreement, nationwide steel strike is called. A settlement is reached between Bethlehem Steel Co. and the United Steelworkers of America which calls for the company-financed continuation of the pension plan and for a jointly-financed welfare plan.

Third largest U.S. steel producer, U.S. Steel signs pension and welfare agreement similar to the one signed earlier by Bethlehem Steel.

The last holdout in steel negotiations, Crucible Steel finally signs contract with the United Steelworkers.

1949 ADVERTISEMENT

How Missouri stays ahead in the Fashion Parade!

ANOTHER AMERICAN AIRFREIGHT SHORT STORY

Nobody has to show Missouri manufacturers *anything* about turning out high-styled shoes, handbags, raincoats and teen-age fashions. And when they saw how airfreight could help them compete successfully with manufacturers located closer to eastern retail centers – the men from Missouri only had to be shown *once*.

Today the business of fashions is flying high in Missouri. Airfreight has helped the St. Louis Fashion Creators continue to grow so rapidly that today they include 115 manufacturers doing an annual wholesale business of over $85,000,000.

Like the apparel makers, many other Midwestern manufacturers are not only using airfreight for faster and more efficient delivery, but also to secure new distribution in territories previously too distant to sell.

Have you stopped to consider how American Airlines Airfreight might help your business grow? For free literature showing the value and versatility of this modern means of distribution, write today to American Airlines, Inc., Cargo Division, 100 E. 42nd St., New York 17, N. Y.

AMERICAN AIRLINES Airfreight

Minimum Wage Is Raised From $.40 To $.75 Per Hour As President Truman Signs The Fair Labor Standards Amendment Of 1949.

The 115-Year Old Long Island Railroad Files A Petition Of Bankruptcy.

Wall Street Remembers Collapse Of The Stock Market 20 Years Ago.

Pillsbury Mills, Inc. Celebrates Its 80th Anniversary With A $100,000 Cooking Contest.

A New $18,000,000 Crucible Steel Company Plant, The First In The Industry Specifically Designed For Cold And Hot Rolling Of Stainless And High-Alloy Sheet And Strip, Opens Outside Of Pittsburgh.

Founder Of The Federation Of Women Shareholders In American Business, Wilma Soss, Predicts That By 1952 Every Big Corporation In America Will Have A Woman On Its Board.

In An Antitrust Suit Filed In Newark, New Jersey, The U.S. Department Of Justice Seeks Separation Of American Telephone And Telegraph Co. From Its Manufacturing Subsidiary, Western Electric Co.

Department Of Justice Files Antitrust Suit Against Du Pont Industrial Giant Calling For Dismantling Their Empire Including The Severance Of Its Connection With General Motors And U.S. Rubber Co.

A Civil Antitrust Suit Is Filed By The U.S. Justice Department Seeking To Divide The Atlantic & Pacific Tea Co. Grocery Chain Into Seven Independent Chains.

The War Assets Administration threatens Chicago automaker **Preston Tucker** with repossession of the Tucker Corp's $170,000,000 plant if he fails to meet his $125,000 rent bill on February 1st.

Conspiracy charges, violation of security act and mail fraud surrounding promotion of Tucker automobiles are leveled against **Preston Tucker** and some of his associates.

Passings

Willard Dow, 52, president of Dow Chemical Company, and his wife Martha, 51, perish in a small plane crash in Canada.

Fruit peddler turned Bank of America founder **Amadeo P. Giannini**, who, as creator of San Francisco's Bank of Italy lent money to small companies, dies at age 79.

Forced to flee his native France during World War II, banker, businessman and race horse owner **Baron Edouard de Rothschild**, who helped raise money for the war effort, dies at age 81.

Inventor **William H. Luden**, who took his successful candies and added menthol, creating the first cough drop, dies at age 90.

With their marketing plans aimed at the pocketbook of the American car buyer, the first International Automobile Show opens in New York City featuring an array of new models from European car makers.

New York gets a look at Hitler's promise to the German people for a "People's Car" which is now produced as the **Volkswagen** at the rate of 3,000 monthly at a German plant.

Cadillac closes its 1949 production line after producing its millionth car, which boasts the fastest acceleration of any stock car capable of going from zero to 80 miles per hour in 23 seconds.

Packard Company celebrates 50 years of manufacturing automobiles.

Chrysler breaks the $1,000,000 sales mark for the first time since 1927.

Installment plans and an increasing number of Americans buying automobiles make this a record year for automobile production. Consumer debt reaches an unprecedented high.

A tubeless tire resistant to blowouts, thus making driving safer, is unveiled by the rubber industry.

THERE MUST BE GOLD IN THAT THERE MAGAZINE

Publisher **Malcolm Forbes** and Editor **Robert Heimann** launch new magazine, *Nation's Heritage*, which is offered at an annual subscription price of $150 or $30 per copy.

DING, DING WENT THE BUS?

PACIFIC ELECTRIC RAILWAY COMPANY REQUESTS PERMISSION OF THE STATE PUBLIC UTILITIES COMMISSION TO PHASE OUT TROLLEYS ON 11 OF ITS 17 STREETCAR ROUTES AND REPLACE THEM WITH BUSES.

The largest public housing program in U.S. history is launched with the passage of President Truman's public housing bill calling for construction of 810,000 units of low-rent housing.

In a move toward normalizing the Japanese economy, the reopening of the Tokyo Stock Exchange is authorized by General Douglas MacArthur.

Visiting British team concludes that American Foundrymen turn out 50% to 90% more work than their British counterparts stating that although the British excel at "the finishing touches" in places where it really counts, Americans are as good as the British.

Britain startles the international community by devaluing the pound 31% from $4.03 to $2.80.

1949 this was the price that was

UNDER $1.00

Anti-Freeze (gallon)	$ 1.00
Chapstick	.25
Coffee	.05
Cola	.05
Cough Drops	.05
Ice Cream Sundae	.40

Lunch at the Russian Tea Room	$ .65
Movie	.85
Paperback Book	.25
Saturday Evening Post	.15
Soap, English Lavender	.45
Staten Island Ferry	.05

HOME NECESSITIES

Cedar Chest	$ 49.95
Chain Saw	95.00
Clock Radio	35.95
Coffeematic coffee maker	24.95
Double Boiler, 2 qt.	8.65
Electric Heater	9.95
Fire Extinguisher	1.25
Flashlight, glow in the dark	1.55
Frying Pan, 10 1/2 in.	7.45
Hair Dryer	7.95
Iron	17.95
Lawn Mower	99.50
Place Setting, sterling silver	28.75
Popcorn Popper, electric	6.95
Radio, portable w/case	49.95
Refrigerator	269.95
Tea Service, 5 piece	$ 132.00
Television	139.95-695.00
Thermometer, outdoor	2.50
Toaster	20.95
Typewriter	84.50
Vacuum	52.50

FOR HIM

Dinner Jacket	$ 27.75
Denim Jeans	3.45
Old Spice After-Shave	1.75
Pajamas	3.95
Robe, silk	25.00
Shirt, cotton oxford	1.95-3.95
Shirt, wool plaid	11.95
Shoes	8.95-16.95
Suspenders	8.50
Trench Coat	13.50

FOR HER

Bathing Suit, 2 piece.....$ 14.95
Beret 3.95
Bra .... 2.00 & up
Dress, silk 49.95
Garter Belt 2.50
Girdle 8.50
Gloves .... 3.50 & up
Hat Box, 16" 13.75
Home Permanent Set.... $ 2.75
Lipstick................. 1.50
Maternity Suit.......... 12.95
Shoes.................. 6.95-20.95
Slacks, Tartan.......... 29.50
Stockings............... 1.35 & up
Suit, Irish Linen........ 39.95
Sweater, Cashmere 16.95

JEWELRY

Tiffany's Brooch, 14k gold . $ 38.00
Cuff Links, gold filled..... 7.50
Diamonds, 1 carat 625.00-1250.00
Necklace, cultured pearl.. 19.95-1500.00
Watch, Babe Ruth 7.95
Watch, 14k gold filled.... 71.50

New York Housing

5 room home in Queens: $11,750
5 room coop in New York City: $4,750
4 room apartment in Bayside: $88.00
3 room apartment in Forest Hills: $110.00

FOOD

Apples, lb. .... $ .13
Butter, lb.................. .73
Coffee, lb. .... .46
Milk, qt.................... .21
Sugar, lb. .... .09
Chocolate, 1 lb. box....... 1.50
Fritos .... .19

AUTOMOBILES

Jaguar .... $ 4,675.00
Kaiser 1,995.00
Oldsmobile 2,586.00
Rolls Royce 14,400.00

1949 ADVERTISEMENT

How are you going to buy your next Car?

The KAISER *Convertible*

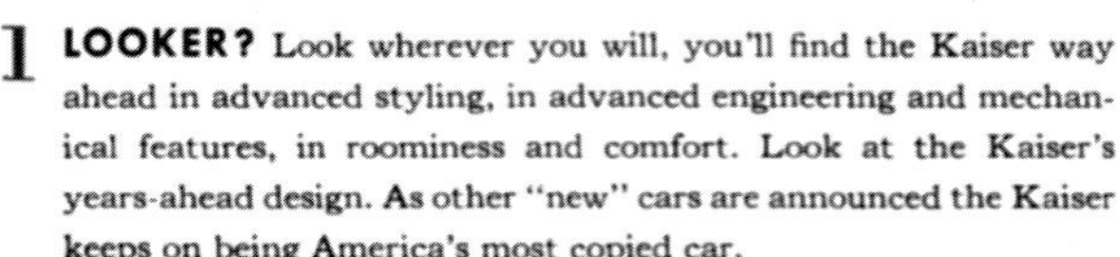

1 LOOKER? Look wherever you will, you'll find the Kaiser way ahead in advanced styling, in advanced engineering and mechanical features, in roominess and comfort. Look at the Kaiser's years-ahead design. As other "new" cars are announced the Kaiser keeps on being America's most copied car.

2 SHOPPER? Shop them all. Let the salesmen tell you their stories. Sure, the Kaiser salesman will be most convincing! Why not? He knows that dollar for dollar his product ***has what it takes***—in economy, in trouble-free performance, in lasting value. More than a quarter-million satisfied owners agree—after more than 3 ***billion*** value-proving owner-driven miles!

The KAISER *Special*

KAISER

4500 KAISER-FRAZER DEALERS INVITE YOU TO—

RIDE - *THEN DECIDE!*

3 DRIVER? Put the Kaiser to every test you know. Learn what the ***highest-compression engine*** in its price class will do. Take the ***roadworthy*** Kaiser over bumps and around curves. A satin-smooth ride, minimum side-sway and vibration! ***Triple-control*** steering brings a new thrill to driving. You'll like it—for keeps!

The KAISER *Virginian—a brand-new idea in motor cars. The smart styling of a convertible under a solid steel roof covered with satin-like nylon.*

Hear! Hear! Hear! *Walter Winchell* Every Sunday...same time...same station!

1949

1949 ADVERTISEMENT

IT'S NEW! IT'S FUN!
NOW THEY'LL LOVE TO BRUSH THEIR TEETH!

Pro-phy-lac-tic
WHISTLE BRUSH
(THERE'S A WHISTLE IN THE HANDLE!)

WHAT a peach of an idea! A child's tooth brush with a two-note whistle built right into the handle! Get one for your youngster today . . . at your drug counter. End-tuft design with natural bristles. Pro-phy-lac-tic Brush Co., *Florence, Mass.*

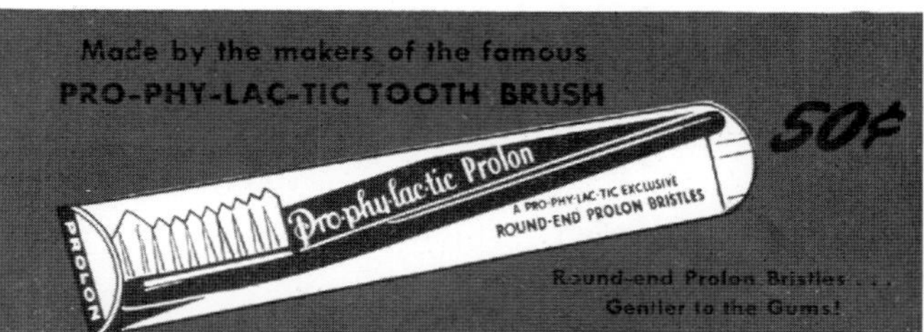

AIRFARE

New York To:

Bermuda	$ 126.00 roundtrip
Cleveland	20.47
Miami	50.00
Los Angeles	99.00
Paris	493.30 roundtrip
Calcutta	1,177.40 roundtrip

BUSFARE (roundtrip)

Chicago to Memphis	$ 15.75
San Francisco to L.A.	10.20
Kansas City to Denver	21.80

ENTERTAINMENT

Boat Rental, Central Park	$ 1.10
Broadway Orchestra Seat	5.00
Hotel Room, Los Angeles	2.25
Hotel Room, Sun Valley	6.00
Monopoly	3.50

WEEKLY SALARIES

Bookkeeper	$ 65.00
Factory Worker	60.00
Keypunch Operator	45.00
Machinist	93.00
Secretary	50.00
Stenographer	40.00
Switchboard Operator	45.00

TOP JOBS

President of the U.S.	$ 100,000.00
Vice President	30,000.00

1949 ADVERTISEMENT

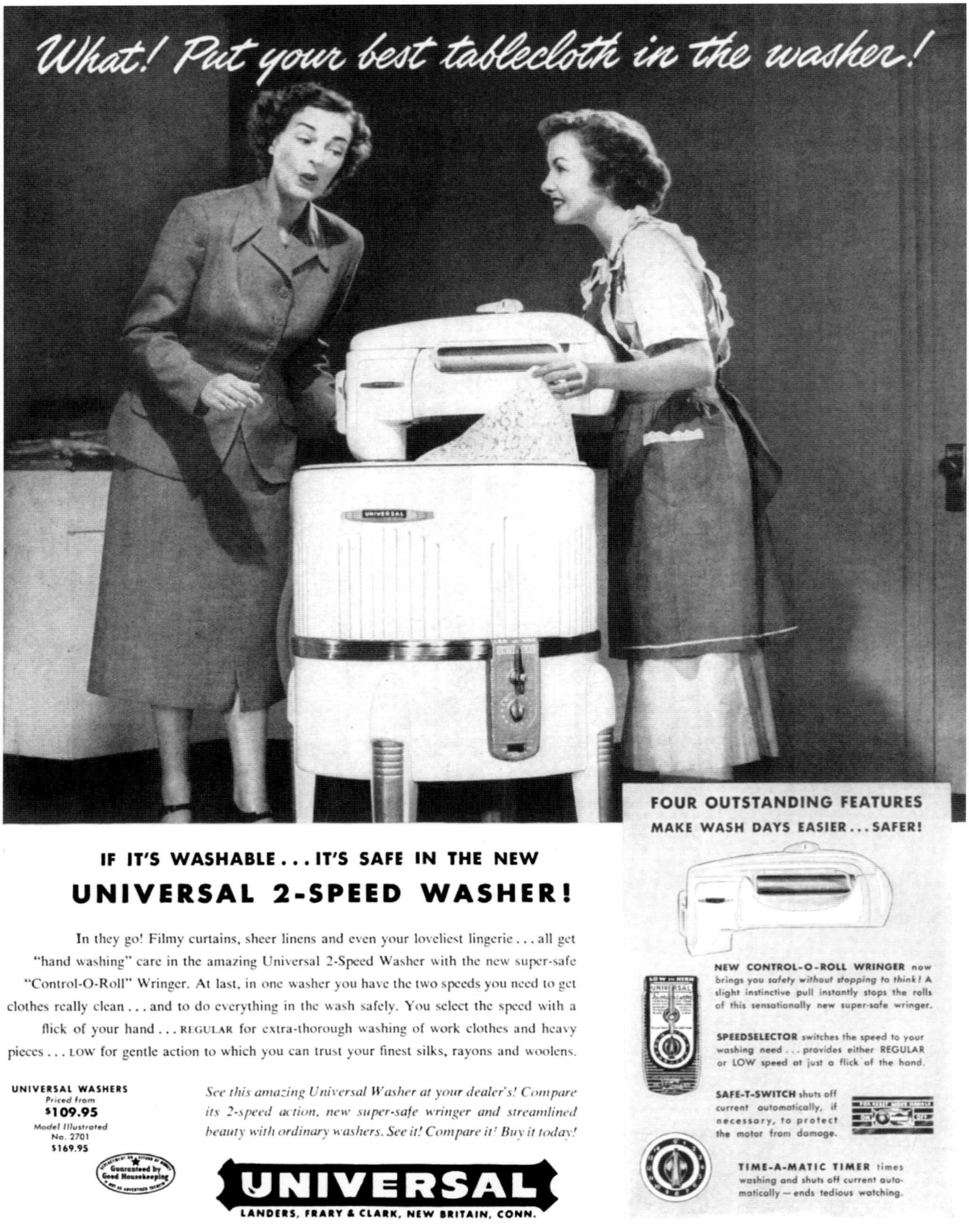

What! Put your best tablecloth in the washer!

FOUR OUTSTANDING FEATURES
MAKE WASH DAYS EASIER . . . SAFER!

IF IT'S WASHABLE . . . IT'S SAFE IN THE NEW
UNIVERSAL 2-SPEED WASHER!

In they go! Filmy curtains, sheer linens and even your loveliest lingerie . . . all get "hand washing" care in the amazing Universal 2-Speed Washer with the new super-safe "Control-O-Roll" Wringer. At last, in one washer you have the two speeds you need to get clothes really clean . . . and to do everything in the wash safely. You select the speed with a flick of your hand . . . REGULAR for extra-thorough washing of work clothes and heavy pieces . . . LOW for gentle action to which you can trust your finest silks, rayons and woolens.

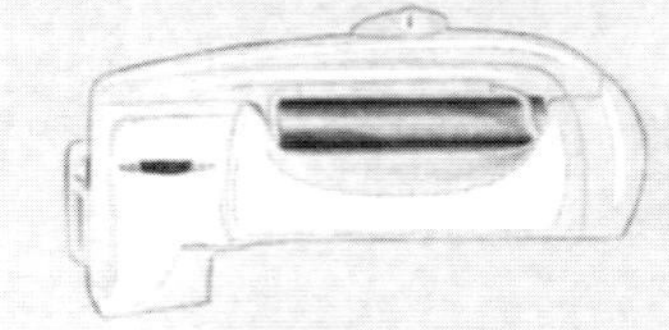

NEW CONTROL-O-ROLL WRINGER now brings you *safety without stopping to think!* A slight instinctive pull instantly stops the rolls of this sensationally new super-safe wringer.

SPEEDSELECTOR switches the speed to your washing need . . . provides either REGULAR or LOW speed at just a flick of the hand.

SAFE-T-SWITCH shuts off current automatically, if necessary, to protect the motor from damage.

TIME-A-MATIC TIMER times washing and shuts off current automatically — ends tedious watching.

UNIVERSAL WASHERS
Priced from
$109.95
Model Illustrated
No. 2701
$169.95

See this amazing Universal Washer at your dealer's! Compare its 2-speed action, new super-safe wringer and streamlined beauty with ordinary washers. See it! Compare it! Buy it today!

1949

SCIENCE & MEDICINE

THE UNITED STATES IS OFFICIALLY IN THE SPACE AGE **with the launching out of White Sands, New Mexico of a 45-foot experimental Navy rocket which reaches a 250-mile altitude.**

ALBERT EINSTEIN is reported to have evolved a generalized theory of gravitation which interrelates all known physical phenomena into a single intellectual concept.

Discovered Over A Year Ago, The Fifth Moon Of The Planet Uranus Is Named Miranda, After The Little Cherub In "The Tempest."

Using the new 48" wide-angle Schmidt photo telescope at the Palomar Observatory in California, the National Geographic Society and California Institute of Technology launch a sky survey to map the reaches of outer space.

After a two-year investigation, the U.S. Air Force officially denies the existence of UFO's.

According to an article appearing in PHYSICS TODAY, the first nuclear rocket propelled by atomic energy is several decades away.

Using the McDonald Observatory's 82-inch telescope, Dr. Gerard P. Kuiper announces the discovery of a possible second satellite for Neptune.

UP, UP AND AWAY

A six-jet Boeing B-47 piloted by majors Russell E. Schleeh and Joseph W. Howell, of the Air Material Command, sets new trans-continental flight record flying from Moses Lake, Washington to Andrews Field, Maryland in 3 hours, 46 minutes.

Carrying 263 passengers and six crew members from San Diego to San Francisco, Navy flying boat Caroline Mars sets new world record for aircraft of any type.

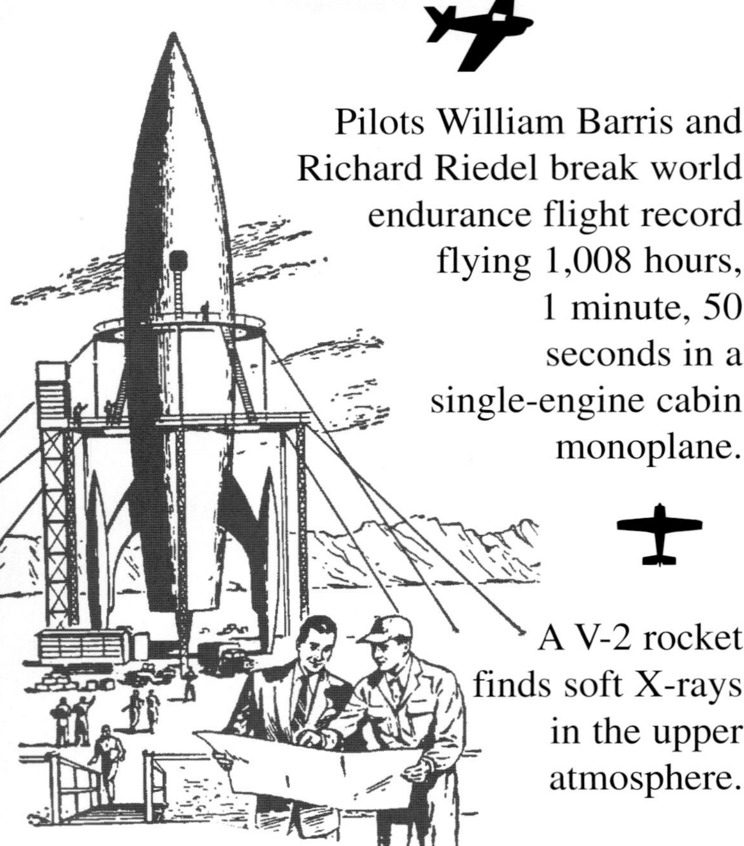

Pilots William Barris and Richard Riedel break world endurance flight record flying 1,008 hours, 1 minute, 50 seconds in a single-engine cabin monoplane.

A V-2 rocket finds soft X-rays in the upper atmosphere.

Los Angeles Airport is first U.S. commercial airport to install and test a fog dispersing system called FIDO designed to allow airliners to land under adverse weather conditions.

The CAA, in conjunction with the Air Force and Navy, adopt a new visual system called "slope line," a funnel-shaped row of lights along the runway, allowing pilots to correctly position their planes during the final stage of approach.

California Institute of Technology announces its "hypersonic" wind tunnel with the fastest air flow ever reached, to be used in studying performances of guided missiles and planes travelling at speeds as high as 5,200 m.p.h.

THIS MAKES HIM SEE RED

Bendix Radio Division, after extensive research, determines that night flying is safer when the radio control panel is illuminated in red, which eliminates glare and minimizes eye fatigue.

Harvard and the University of California Medical School construct new atom smashers.

Claiming possession of an atomic bomb since 1947, the Soviets detonate their first atomic device resulting in thousands of Americans participating in "Operation Skywatch," scanning the skies for Soviet bombers.

According to testimony given to the House Un-American Activities Committee, under orders from Harry L. Hopkins uranium and atomic bomb data had been flown to the USSR in 1943 and 1944.

Following on the heels of a congressional investigation of the Atomic Energy Commission, the AEC will now be required to obtain a loyalty oath from recipients of fellowships, and atomic energy contracts awarded by Congress will be more closely scrutinized.

According to the British Ministry of Supply, Britain is producing plutonium for the first time.

The development of the "breeder reactor," an atomic reactor that produces more energy than it uses, is announced.

Using the vibrations of nitrogen atoms, the development of an atomic clock, which will not gain or lose more than one second in three million years, is announced by the National Bureau of Standards.

W.F. Libby and James Arnold of the University of Chicago develop a system of dating certain kinds of archaeological remains using the radioactivity of the carbon isotope, Carbon 14.

NOW LET'S SEE, WHERE DID I PUT THAT THING

A small amount of missing uranium is confirmed by the U.S. Atomic Energy Commission although it denies that it has been stolen or lost from the Argon Atomic Laboratory in Chicago.

OH THERE YOU ARE

Four months after the disappearance of a bottle containing uranium, the Atomic Energy Commission announces it found the bottle at a dump for radioactive nuclear waste.

Fertilized Ova From Artificially Inseminated Pedigreed Cows Are Successfully Implanted In The Bodies Of Scrub Cows.

Larger Yield Of Milk In The Spring May Be Due To A Female Sex Hormone Present In Fresh, Young Spring Grass.

A New Cattle Disease Called "X" Threatens Cattle Herds In Over Thirty States.

- The first photograph of a gene magnified 120,000 times is produced by Drs. Daniel Pease and Richard Baker.

- The traditional designation "degrees Centigrade" has been changed to "degrees Celsius" with the consent of scientists representing 28 nations.

- A pueblo house dating back to about A.D. 900 is discovered in western New Mexico, making it the earliest-known example of a masonry house.

- Westinghouse Electric Corp. announces the development of the world's lightest solid–a plastic foam to be used as refrigerator insulant.

Micrografting is used to save valuable hybrid plants that can't break through the seed coat.

New research on photosynthesis reveals that under favorable conditions 65% of absorbed light energy can be transformed into chemical energy by green cells.

Why Are Strawberries Red, Daddy?

Scientists at the New York Agricultural Experiment Station at Geneva, New York isolate anthocyanin as the reason strawberries are red and suggest that a bright red color usually means good flavor and a high vitamin C content.

Bees Turn Their Backs On Red

During a lecture at the Museum of Natural History, Austrian scientist Dr. Karl von Frisch reveals that his continuing research with bees produced evidence that bees have a highly developed color sense and avoid red blossoms almost completely, preferring the nectar from blue, green, white or ultra-violet flowers.

A Sticky Situation

According to the U.S. Department of Agriculture, Gelsoy, a new substance found in soybeans, can be used in a variety of ways from whipped cream to glue.

This Is For The Birds

Research on how human beings learn to speak is being conducted at the University of Illinois by teaching birds to speak, revealing that before a bird will talk, it must have the care and affection of its trainer, much the same as a baby needs the love and attention of its mother.

Successful testing of Aureomycin makes it the first drug for the treatment of viral pneumonia.

New Meaning To Lover's Triangle

Brown University biologist Paul B. Weisz announces Blepharisma, a 1/100 of an inch long one-cell animal, has a complex sex life as it comes in three sexes—A, B and C. During mating Cell A simultaneously fertilizes Cell B, B fertilizes C and C completes the triangle by fertilizing A.

Blow Off Some Steam Honey, You'll Feel Better

For women who suffer from a general malaise and are not sick, Dr. Irving D. Harris, of the Institute for Juvenile Research in Chicago, suggests that they lose their temper once in a while to vent suppressed feelings of anger.

Kisses Sweeter Than Sugar

Monsanto Chemical 'fesses up that the reason some kisses are so sweet is due to the presence of saccharin in some lipsticks.

Anthropologist **Margaret Mead** states in her book Male And Female *"...the human female's capacity for orgasm is to be viewed much more as a potentiality that may or may not be developed by a given culture."*

FUTURE EINSTEINS OF THE WORLD

SCIENCE CLUBS OF AMERICA, which conducts the annual science talent search for the Westinghouse Science Scholarships, now boasts 15,000 affiliated clubs in the United States and abroad with a third of a million participating girls and boys.

Not Just A Flash In The Pan, By Zeus

At the world's largest man-made lightning center at General Electric, the most powerful lightning bolts ever created by man are engineered at the new High Voltage Engineering Laboratory.

It's Your Move, RO-BO

In his recent book Cybernetics, brilliant mathematician and electronic robot authority, Professor Norbert Wiener of the Massachusetts Institute of Technology, states that he believes it is possible to construct a chess-playing machine that would play through all its own possible moves and all its opponent's moves for two or three moves ahead.

Engineers at the California Institute of Technology develop an almost unbeatable TicTacToe machine.

I CAN'T SLEEP—THE PINK WALLS ARE KEEPING ME UP

New research reveals bright cheerful colors such as pink, yellow or orange, long favorites for bedrooms, may actually produce disturbing effects while the more subtle blues and greens are more conducive to a good night's sleep.

With regard to giving potential employees an intelligence test, the JOURNAL OF APPLIED PSYCHOLOGY reports that these tests should be used for clerical workers and not sales clerks as the test scores are actually inversely related to effectiveness as a sales clerk.

A professor at Chicago's Loyola University did a survey on why students cheat and here are some of the reasons:

- Resentment of too much emphasis on grades as a measure of performance.
- Fear of failing and consequently losing G.I. Bill of Rights benefits.
- Fear of falling short of family expectations.
- Necessity of a good scholastic record for future employment.
- "My friends do it and I have to compete by getting as good or better grades."

A BENTHOSCOPE MANNED BY OTIS BARTON REACHES RECORD DEEP-SEA DIVE OF 4,500 FEET OFF SOUTHERN CALIFORNIA COAST.

THE PORT OF LONG BEACH, CALIFORNIA INSTALLS A RADAR-CONTROL SYSTEM TO FACILITATE SHIP MOVEMENT IN INCLEMENT WEATHER USING WALKIE-TALKIE RADIOS.

Funded by a $100,000 grant from the Rockefeller Foundation, the University of California at Berkeley launches study into why some people fail while others succeed.

THE FOUNTAIN OF YOUTH MADE SIMPLE

Thanks to Allied influence, the Japanese Diet is discarding its traditional way of computing ages—which makes a baby one year old when it's born—and is adopting the Western method, which will make every Japanese man, woman and child from one to two years younger at the end of this year, depending on date of birth.

The U.S. State Department grants permission to 23 European Eastern Bloc countries to send delegates to the Cultural and Scientific Conference for World Peace in New York. Opening session heavily picketed by veterans and religious groups denouncing the conference as a communist sounding board.

SOME LIKE IT HOT

According to studies conducted at the University of Minnesota, a large helping of cold ice cream will cool you off but an equal amount of hot ice cream will not warm you up.

FOR MEDICINAL PURPOSES ONLY

In his address to the **Doctor Friends of Wine** at their meeting in Bordeaux, France, Paris physician Dr. Raymond Wissenbach tells the gathering that in order to maintain good health, laborers should drink more than a quart of wine daily while the intellectual needs only a little

THIS WILL MAKE YOUR HAIR CURL

Doctors give cold-wave home permanents a clean bill of health absolving them from any negative side effects.

JUST A BUNCH OF GIBBERISH

According to a professor at the Massachusetts Institute of Technology, between 10% to 100% of the average American's communication contains virtually no information.

DROP THAT SNOWBALL

The *Yale Journal of Biology and Medicine* carries a warning that rubbing snow on frostbite causes rather than prevents gangrene and that a treatment of rapid thawing and application of Tetraethylammonium should be administered immediately.

I've Been Working On The Railroad And I'm A Nervous Wreck

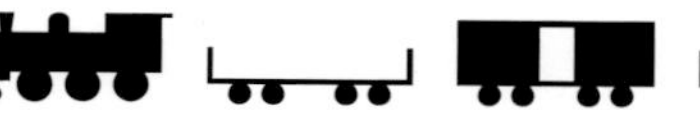

Research reveals that the most nerve-wracking job is that of a train dispatcher who pulls the throttle on 20-50 trains and is called on to exercise vital judgement at the rate of 200 decisions per hour.

A Study Conducted At The University Of Chicago Reveals That Highly Prejudiced People Generally Hate Themselves.

LIFE IN THE BIG CITY

Passive recreational activities such as listening to the radio, reading or watching television inhibits recovery from serious illnesses suffered by patients living in cities vs. their country counterparts who have to meet the daily needs of living on a farm.

1949

Rx

- Philip Hench discovers Cortisone.
- Cortisone found to be effective in controlling arthritis through daily doses which takes 40 head of cattle to supply.
- Neomycin isolated by Selman Waksman.
- Drs. Emanuel B. Schoenbach and Morton S. Bryer of Baltimore announce the new golden-colored antibiotic, Aureomycin, is effective against primary atypical pneumonia which has resisted all other drugs.
- Dramamine, introduced by G.D. Searle & Company for motion sickness, is also found effective in relieving side effects of X-ray and radium therapy as well as morning sickness in pregnant women.
- A new vaccine called BCG, believed to build up immunity to tuberculosis in people not already infected, begins wide-scale testing in the United States.
- Lithium is used for the first time in the treatment of psychiatric disorders.
- The hormone FSH, which holds the key to fertility in both men and women, has been isolated in pure form for the first time.
- Refills of prescriptions without physician authorization will become a thing of the past as the U.S. Food and Drug Administration launches a drive to end this practice.
- For the first time in history, Parke, Davis and Company has synthesized an antibiotic similar to penicillin called Chloromycetin for use in treating various diseases including Rocky Mountain spotted fever, pneumonia, typhus fever, typhoid fever, viral pneumonia and whooping cough.
- A powerful new drug called Bacitracin is quite effective in treating a multitude of skin and eye infections with virtually no side effects.
- A new drug made of procaine penicillin in oil and aluminum is developed that is safe, easy to use, inexpensive and effective in the treatment of syphilis.
- Glutamic Acid has been found effective in raising mental age of Mongoloid children.
- Chemists develop a pill called Coricidin purported to kill the common cold.
- A report appears in the Journal of the American Medical Association that daily prophylactic doses of penicillin does not prevent colds.
- Dexedrine, a new form of Benzedrine, found effective as appetite suppressant.

the CANCER front

- Vitamin B-14, which in test tube tests stops the growth of certain cancer tissues, is discovered by two researchers at the University of Washington, Earl R. Norris and John Majnarich.
- The American Cancer Society issues a report linking the growing incidences of lung cancer over the past 25 years to cigarette smoking.
- Heading a chemical group from the California Institute of Technology, Dr. Linus Pauling discovers sickle-cell anemia as the world's first molecular disease.
- British Columbia starts a screening program to detect pre-invasive carcinoma of the cervix.
- The New York Memorial Cancer Center receives $2,000,000 donation from John D. Rockefeller, Jr.
- The first atomic-smasher built as a medical device now offers cancer patients a new radiation treatment that penetrates deeper than conventional X-rays without damaging surface tissue is now available to cancer patients at the University of Illinois.
- Dr. Charles B. Huggins, of the University of Chicago, announces the development of a simple but reasonably accurate blood test for detecting cancer.
- At a conference on sex hormones and breast cancer in Chicago, Dr. Walton van Winkle, Jr. suggests the male hormone testosterone be used in women with inoperable breast cancer.

Cases of poliomyelitis reach record high in the U.S.

According to an article appearing in the A.M.A. Journal, cold rather than heat is recommended in treatment of poisonous bites and stings.

Dr. Clemens E. Benda, instructor in neuropathology at Harvard Medical School, concludes that Mongolism idiocy is not inherited but rather is a decelerating growth deficiency.

KNEE-JERK REACTION

If you are between 6 and 20 years old, how fast your foot jerks forward when the doctor strikes your knee is directly proportional to your height.

The National Heart Institute awards grants for heart disease research amounting to more than $1,200,000 to medical schools and hospitals in the United States and Canada.

SURGICAL ADVANCES

Hoping to plug color television for home use, CBS to give first long look at their latest technology at the annual meeting of the American Medical Association in Atlantic City, where 100,000 doctors will see via closed circuit, made possible through the use of a specially built color camera, operations being performed at the University of Pennsylvania's medical school.

The use of a plastic false lung shaped into a bag and filled with fiberglass is under experimentation at the Mayo Clinic.

Physicians at Wayne University seeking a non-amputation treatment for gangrene develop an operation which "runs the blood in reverse" and involves sewing an artery end-to-end with a vein.

A new device is developed which is designed to electrically massage the heart during heart surgery.

MICROWAVE ENERGY may provide a safe, convenient source of therapeutic heat for treatment of arthritis, bursitis and muscle inflammation.

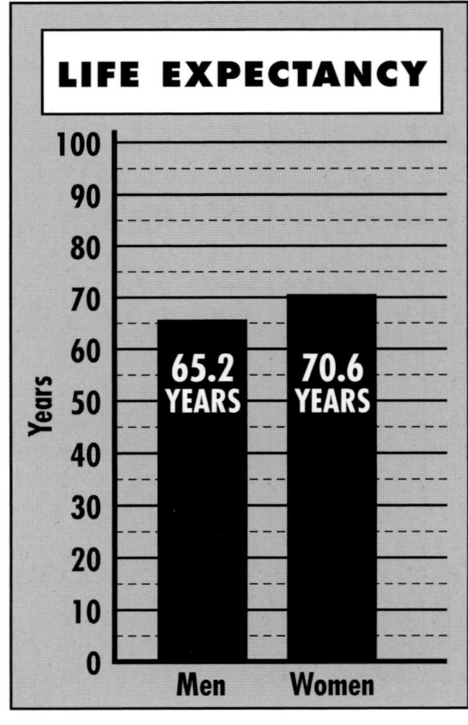

- Biologists John Enders, Thomas Weller and Frederick Robbins cultivate poliovirus in vitro on human embryonic tissue.
- The National Institute of Public Health is established.
- Largest member of AMA, the New York County Medical Society, refuses to support AMA's fight against President Truman's compulsory medical insurance proposal.
- Progress is made in photosynthesis research in determining the intermediates in the chemical reactions by which the green plant under the influence of sunlight converts CO_2 and H_2O into O_2.
- The first International Conference of Diabetes Associations is held in Brussels.

PSYCHIATRY

Psychiatrists are using a new test developed by Dr. Renatus Hartogs of the Allan Memorial Institute of Psychiatry in Montreal whereby the patient draws a person which helps the doctor diagnose the mental illness.

Minnesota becomes first state to enact a law recognizing mental illness as a sickness.

People who have phobias generally have not matured emotionally, according to a New Canaan, Connecticut doctor.

WHATEVER HAPPENED TO THE LITTLE OLD WHITE LIE?

ACCORDING TO AN ARTICLE APPEARING IN THE PSYCHIATRIC QUARTERLY, THERE ARE 8 VARIETIES OF LIES:

BENIGN LIES	LIES FOR THE SAKE OF POLITENESS
COMPENSATORY LIES	COVERS UP FEELINGS OF INSECURITY
DEFENSIVE LIES	TO GET OUT OF A TIGHT SPOT
GOSSIP	TO DELIBERATELY HURT SOMEONE
HYSTERICAL LIES	TO GET ATTENTION OR SYMPATHY
IMPLIED LIES	WITHHOLD TRUTH THROUGH SILENCE
LOVE LIES	WHISPERING SWEET NOTHINGS
PATHOLOGICAL LIES	STEMMING FROM FANTASIES AND DELUSIONS

Love is the key to good mental and emotional health.

Psychologists believe that accident-prone people tend to be emotionally maladjusted with a symptom of neurosis, the result of an unconscious urge to self-injury.

NOTHING TO SNEEZE AT

Studies of the mentally ill show that they generally do not suffer from hay fever.

Dr. Henry A. Schroeder of Washington University School of Medicine reports that contrary to popular opinion, the high blood pressure personality is not the explosive, desk-pounding type, but rather the mild, non-assertive person with obsessive-compulsive traits, such as double or triple checking to make sure he has turned out the lights or locked the door.

Studies show that a nervous breakdown is less likely to be precipitated by overwork than by unemployment or fear of unemployment.

NOBEL PRIZES

MEDICINE & PHYSIOLOGY
Walter Rudolf Hess (Switzerland)
and
Antonio Caetano de Abreu Freire Egas Moniz (Portugal)

PHYSICS
Hideki Yukawa (Japan)

CHEMISTRY
William Francis Giauque (U.S.A.)

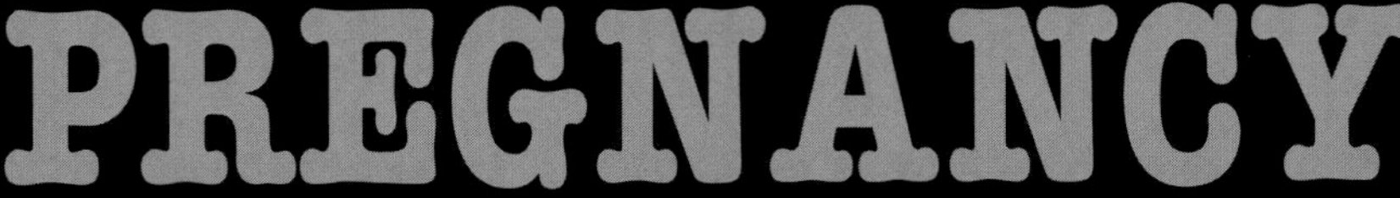

Cornell University studies indicate that when kings and queens marry within their own family, the intelligence level of the children is generally lower than that of children born to people who marry outside their family.

Menstrual pain and accidental abortions have been shown to be allergic reactions to one of the body's hormones called Vasopressin.

DUKE UNIVERSITY'S Drs. Deryl Hart and James D. Moody work on a controversial theory that the time of conception in relation to a woman's menstrual cycle has an important bearing on the sex of a child.

PHYSICIANS BEGIN DOING ROUTINE BLOOD TESTING of pregnant women to determine the presence or absence of the Rh factor to avoid stillbirths and certain types of fatal anemia in newborns.

HEMORRHAGING is #1 cause of death in pregnant women.

AN ACCURATE URINE TEST for pregnancy is developed by Dr. Garwood Richardson of Northwestern University.

THE FRIEDMAN TEST to determine if a pregnancy exists is developed whereby a small amount of urine is injected into a rabbit who in two days will yield the results.

JAPAN officially sanctions birth control.

NUTRITION

Older people will live longer with balanced nutrition including milk according to Dr. Clive M. McCay, professor of nutrition at Cornell University who states that the study of nutrition could contribute greatly toward solving the problem of aging.

Human beings require eight "essential" amino acids in their diet, according to William Cunning Rose, and the body can use them to compensate for other deficiencies.

Studies reveal small quantities of DDT in cow's milk and the Food and Drug Administration calls for stricter regulations of dairy barns so as not to permit any direct contamination of milk by this toxic substance.

In laboratory experiments at New York's Fordham University, rats on high-protein diets show signs of disease faster than those on low-protein foods. It is concluded that people who eat meat and eggs should balance their diet with vitamin B-6 which is available in vegetable fats, whole-grain cereals, legumes and yeast.

For those people who work under a strain or are convalescing from an illness, it is wise to take a half hour rest before meals which will aid in proper digestion.

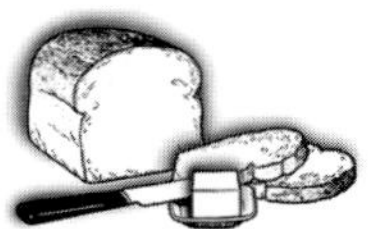

The use of preservatives in bread to extend freshness is viewed with considerable caution by the Council on Foods and Nutrition of the American Medical Association.

Sorry Popeye—Next Time Pop Open A Can Of Kale

Despite popular belief, spinach is not a superior source of strength and energy as it is low in iron and calcium. A better source? Kale.

Doctors issue a warning that the hamburger, America's favorite food, must be cooked "very well done" to avoid danger of trichinosis from miscellaneous scraps of pork which might be thrown into the chopped meat unbeknownst to the customer.

How Did You Say You Wanted Your Polar Bear Burger?

Travelers to the far north are warned to make sure their polar bear meat and walrus meat are well done in order to avoid trichinosis.

According to tests conducted by Drs. James F. Rinehart and Louis D. Greenberg of the University of California Medical School, the basic cause of arteriosclerosis may be lack of vitamin B-6.

Research begins on the elucidation of the structure of vitamin B-12.

The practice of osteopathy celebrates its 75th anniversary.

Presently being used to detect flaws in metal, ultrasound may now be used to locate gallstones and other foreign matter inside the human body according to Dr. George D. Ludwig of the Naval Research Medical Institute in Washington, D.C. where he has been experimenting with ultrasound on animals.

Designed to wean polio patients off the respirator, the National Foundation for Infantile Paralysis funds the development of a new rocking or tilting bed which moves up and down automatically with the patient's respiration. Initial tests at the Willard Parker Hospital on New York's East River prove successful.

A new device built by the Allis-Chalmers Manufacturing Co. allows patient suffering from uremic poisoning to undergo treatment which pumps blood from his body through cellophane tubing wound around a revolving drum allowing poison to be filtered through the cellophane and the healthy blood to return to the patient's body.

A new device allowing doctors to see as well as hear a heartbeat is developed by the faculty of the New York University-Bellevue Medical Center.

84-year old Dr. Andy Hall of Mount Vernon, Illinois, in rural general practice for 60 years, is recognized as Doctor of the Year by the American Medical Association.

Dr. William A. Hinton, named Clinical Professor of Bacteriology and Immunology, becomes first Negro to hold a professorship at Harvard University.

Mayo Clinic's Dr. Edward C. Kendall reports success in treating arthritis with a combination of a hormone from the adrenal glands of cattle and the natural pituitary hormone ACTH.

A Hug A Day Could Keep TB Away

In a study conducted by Eric Wittkower of 785 tuberculosis patients concerning emotional factors contributing to this disease, he discovers that an inordinate need for affection is an outstanding common feature of the personality of these patients.

The Journal of the American Medical Association issues a report stating that scientific evidence does not substantiate the belief that children born of tubercular parents have a hereditary susceptibility to the disease.

A warning is issued by the National Society for the Prevention of Blindness that wearing sunglasses too much for that "Movie Star Image" or looking directly at the sun could cause serious eye problems.

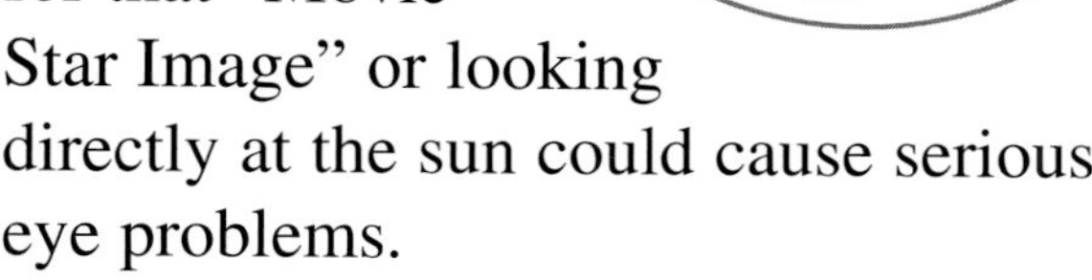

The American Optical Company designs shatter-proof lenses for active children.

In order to avoid eye strain when watching television, a six or seven foot distance from the screen is recommended.

SPECIAL RECOGNITION

Dr. Oswald Avery
Rockefeller Institute for Medical Research
(Isolation and classification of pneumonia germs into four types)

Dr. Benjamin Pasamanik
Kings County Hospital
(Study showing Negroes have same mental capacity as other races)

AMA Distinguished Service Award
Seale Harris
Birmingham, Alabama

Andre Cournand
(Physiology of circulation and the diagnosis and treatment of heart disease)

William S. Tillett & L.S. Christensen
(Discovery and purification of stretokinase and streptokinase enzymes)

Max Theiler
(Experiments leading to the production of two effective vaccines against yellow fever)

Edward C. Kendall & Philip S. Hench
(Chemical, physiological and clinical studies of adrenal hormones culminating in the use of cortisone in rheumatic disease therapy)

George M. Cooper
(Maternal and child health)

Mildred C. Scoville
(Integration of mental health concepts in medical education and practice)

Albert Deutsch
(Advancement of mental health through books, magazine and newspaper articles)

The Florence Nightingale Award (Nursing)
Alta Elizabeth Dines
Mary M. Roberts

1949 ADVERTISEMENT

- THE FASTEST PORTABLE IN THE WORLD!
- THE SMOOTHEST WRITING PORTABLE EVER BUILT!
- THE FIRST PORTABLE WITH Colorspeed KEYBOARD!
- THE WORLD'S MOST ADVANCED PORTABLE DESIGN!
- ALL NEW PLUS SMITH-CORONA "KNOW HOW"

THE NEW 1950 SMITH-CORONA PORTABLE

SILENT

Smith-Corona

THREE NEW MODELS:

Silent (illustrated) $89.50, Sterling $84.50, Clipper $79.50, in all states having "fair trade" laws. Prices are exclusive of taxes and are subject to revision. Ask about terms.

NEW! EXCLUSIVE!

INTRODUCING

Colorspeed

KEYBOARD

Full size, Standard Office Keyboard. Molded key tops are specially shaped to fit your fingers. Harmonious green colors are restful to eyes. Characters will not wear off. It brings a new "touch" to typing. Type faster, easier, with less fatigue.

PLUS THESE NEW TYPING AIDS

Quickset Margin Control
Synchronized Carriage Return
Line Spacer
Frame-Fit Space Bar
3-Way Paper Bail
Retractable Paper Supports
and many others

At last! A PORTABLE WITH THE TOUCH AND ACTION OF AN OFFICE TYPEWRITER!

The 1950 Smith-Corona is not just a new model or "improved" machine. It has been completely redesigned inside and out, and introduces many "first time" typing features. Its Revolutionary *Super-Speed* Escapement and Dual Universal Action are mainly responsible for its lighter, "snappier" touch and amazing speed.

No wonder the new Smith-Corona has been hailed, "the fastest, smoothest writing portable in the world."

L C SMITH & CORONA TYPEWRITERS INC SYRACUSE I N Y ©1949

Give THE ALL-NEW 1950 SMITH-CORONA IT'S THE PERFECT CHRISTMAS GIFT!

NEW PRODUCTS AND INVENTIONS

The first Polaroid Land Camera which produces a photograph in 60 seconds hits the market.

A box camera loaded with film both of which the user forwards for development is being marketed by a Dallas Company.

A technique for taking underwater motion pictures at depths of as much as 100 feet is developed by the British Admiralty.

Owners of cars illegally parked in Denver might be surprised to find their wheels clamped with a new invention that immobilizes the car.

Chrysler introduces the key ignition on some of its models which replaces the button ignition.

A green plexiglass visor which extends the entire width of an automobile windshield designed to cut sun and headlight glare is introduced by the Western Plastic Service of Great Falls, Montana.

The U.S. Rubber Co. develops a scuff-proof white sidewall tire.

HONEY, DID YOU DEFROST THE COFFEE YET?

For $.47 a can that yields 30 cups of coffee, housewives can for the first time buy coffee in a frozen concentrate similar to frozen orange juice.

A one-cup coffee bag, much like a tea bag, has been introduced by the Per Cup Coffee Corp. of Boston.

The Italian Necchi sewing machine introduces the first zig-zag stitch.

The left-handed can now buy watches, pens, corkscrews, scissors and checkbooks designed just for them.

Stick Your Money Up Your Mitt!

A glove with a small zippered pocket built into the palm of the left hand and big enough to hold change, a key and a few dollars is now available thanks to the Regina Glove Company.

Machine washable wool blankets soon to be available.

PUT AWAY THOSE MIXING BOWLS, HONEY

Three inventors in St. Louis come up with the idea of putting cream into a bomb similar to the ones used for dispensing DDT to allow housewives to have instant whipped cream.

★★★★★★★★★★★★★★★★★★★★★★★★★★★

A new double-bladed spatula hits the market capable of turning eggs, pancakes, etc. without breaking or slipping, with a lower blade for picking up the food and fork-shaped upper blade for holding it steady.

★★★★★★★★★★★★★★★★★★★★★★★★★★★

A toaster that automatically shuts off and pops up the toast is invented by the Sunbeam Corporation in Chicago.

★★★★★★★★★★★★★★★★★★★★★

HITTING THE BOILING POINT

A coil embedded in a Pyrex kettle that boils a quart of water in five minutes is invented by Dr. Peter Schlumbohm.

★★★★★★★★★★★★★★★★★★★★★★★★★★★

HAVE DIRTY DISHES, WILL TRAVEL

A new portable dishwashing machine that sits on the drainboard of a sink is available for $89.95.

★★★★★★★★★★★★★★★★★★★★★★★★★★★

GENERAL MILLS COMES UP WITH A HALF-BAKED IDEA

Housewives can now buy rolls that have been pre-baked and all they have to do is stick them in the oven and heat them up.

★★★★★★★★★★★★★★★★★★

General Mills and Pillsbury introduce cake mixes.

★★★★★★★★★★★★★★★★★★

For your sweet tooth, Sara Lee introduces her newest wonder, cheesecake.

★★★★★★★★★★★★★★★★★★★★★★★★★★★

If your man gets the munchies during the baseball game, you can offer him a bowl of Chee-tos.

LADIES NO LONGER have to be quite as concerned with crooked seams thanks to Miss Lillian Bernstein, a Boston secretary who came up with the idea of putting a tiny rubber pad with a slot that the garter fits into between the stocking and the leg.

SECRETARIES CAN NOW know when they should stop typing on a page with the development of an electrical warning device that signals as the end of the page nears.

BUT WHAT IF IT GETS DARK?

The U.S. Navy and the National Bureau of Standards invent a new non-magnetic compass known as the "Sky Compass" which works off of sunlight.

THE U.S. ARMY SIGNAL CORPS Base at Ft. Monmouth, N.J. unveils a no-echo chamber designed and constructed to test delicate instruments.

A BLOB of bouncing silicone is turned into "Silly Putty" by a Connecticut entrepreneur named Peter Hodgson.

THE TINY BINAC, the world's second largest all-electronic automatic calculator capable of calculating 12,000 times faster than a human is demonstrated by its inventors, Dr. John W. Mauchly and Presper Eckert, Jr.

No More Shocking Experiences

The "No-Shok" electric outlet is developed by the Bell Electric Company.

Sears, Roebuck & Co. is featuring an illuminated light switch which is activated when the light is turned off.

Less Work For Mother

Disposable coated paper plates are now available for those Sunday picnics.

Hello, Is This A Machine To Whom I Am Speaking?

A telephone answering device has been developed by the Mohawk Business Machines Corp. of New York which lifts the receiver off the hook, plays a recording saying you're not home and then records a message.

A ***miniature portable typewriter*** with a modified keyboard using stenography abbreviations is developed by a company in San Diego, California.

A ***new slow-speed airplane*** that can land and take off from an area no bigger than a tennis court is designed by a professor at Massachusetts Institute of Technology.

T*he National Electronic Conference* in Chicago witnesses the unveiling of a new sound-tape copying machine developed by Minnesota Mining & Manufacturing.

A ***toothbrush*** with built-in toothpaste is being marketed by Consumers' Shoppers of Kingston, New York.

A ***precooked packaged dessert*** that is ready in less than a minute is introduced in New York.

INSTANT UP IN FLAMES

A fire log which ignites without the use of kindling and burns for about an hour is introduced by the Kindle-Lite Corp. of Brooklyn, New York.

A ***process is developed*** for canning fresh milk without changing the flavor.

A ***special chair*** with built-in telephone table and shelf for a phone book makes talking on the phone for hours very comfortable—especially for teenagers.

SHADES OF THINGS TO COME

The American Optical Company of Southbridge, Mass., develops a sunglass lens which eliminates both ultraviolet rays and reflected sunlight. The company is researching adapting this new lens to non-prescription sunglasses.

ROLL OUT THE BARRELS

T*he British invent a beer gun* which forces the beer through a flexible tube in the gun.

Cleaning Your Water And Drinking It, Too
A home water filter device is introduced by the Mansfield Aqua-Mite Filter Co. of Chicago.

No More Slipping And Sliding
A nonslip floor polish for hardwood and gymnasium floors is developed by the Walter G. Legge Co. of New York.

Learning To Ride A Bike Without Falling
A bicycle with two tricycle-like balancing wheels designed for children ages 3 to 7 is being manufactured by the Huffman Manufacturing Co. of Dayton, Ohio.

An automobile-type headlight for bicycles is developed by General Electric.

A ***voltmeter*** that can test the life of a battery is developed by Socony-Vacuum Oil Co.

T***he famous Toni Twins*** are now available in twin doll sets complete with a cold-wave kit for dressing up the tresses.

A ***hidden latch*** for cabinets which can open when touched lightly is developed by the National Lock Co. of Rockford, Illinois.

A ***12-pound*** portable radio-phonograph designed for the new 45 RPM records and capable of playing eight records continuously is offered by Motorola, Inc. of Chicago.

K***iddies can now*** make their own recordings with a recording toy developed by General Electric.

A ONE-MAN ENTERTAINMENT CENTER

A new musical instrument is developed by the Trio-Art Piano Company of Philadelphia which includes a piano with electronic amplification, automatic phonograph, public address system, recorder and AM and FM radio.

T***he United States Air Force*** develops a heat-resistant ceramic for use in jet and rocket engines.

A ***disposable oxygen mask*** for airline passengers to use in case of an emergency has been developed and is being tested at the Wright Patterson Air Force base. The mask is expected to be effective at altitudes up to 25,000 feet.

WOULD YOU MIND REPEATING THAT AGAIN?

Small enough to put in two briefcases, the first mobile wire recorder, which can pick up sounds within twenty feet, is developed by Russell D. Mason, a Los Angeles sound technician.

architecture + design

Eero Saarinen and Charles Eames join forces to build a case study house.

Ground is broken for over 1 million U.S. residences—a record high.

Realtor William Zeckendorf devises a cost-efficient circular apartment house and hires I.M. Pei to further the idea.

National Homes Corporation's prefabricated two bedroom abodes, with lot, sell for under $6,000.

The garden of New York's Museum of Modern Art is the setting for Marcel Breuer's contemporary family house, planned with future additions in mind, for folks who commute to city jobs.

Frank Lloyd Wright receives the American Institute of Architects' Gold Medal for being a "titanic force" in the field. Wright, honored to receive the award, is not a member of the organization.

Historic buildings are given a respite from destruction as Congress approves the National Trust for Historic Preservation.

The **Henri Matisse** conceived Church Sainte Marie du Rosaire begins construction in the south of France.

In Connecticut PHILIP C. JOHNSON erects his own glass house, virtually bringing the outdoors into his living space. The furniture is created by architect MIES VAN DER ROHE.

The MIES VAN DER ROHE designed Illinois Institute of Technology is completed.

The Ranch style is a favorite for private dwellings.

Richard Nuetra designs a contemporary home with sleek lines and lots of glass in Palm Springs, California. It wins the "Distinguished Award" from the Southern California chapter of the American Institute of Architects.

1949

Salvador Dali

is one of several artists chosen to create new hand-screened fabrics for furniture.

THE FIRST ANNUAL PACIFIC COAST DECORATIVE ARTS
competition is held at the San Francisco Museum of Art.

The Museum of Modern Art in New York holds a furniture design competition, and receives 3,000 entries from over 30 countries.

CITRON YELLOW, **NAVY BLUE**, **CHARCOAL PURPLE** and **AVOCADO GREEN** are some of the year's choicest decorating colors.

Plastic products are helping your home look spiffy and modern in every room. Furniture fabrics made of plastic include **Lumite**, **Pandanus**, **Duran**, **Boltaflex** and **Nylon**. Their advantage? Easy to clean, resistance to stains, and a long life. Flooring of **Formica**, **Koroseal** and **Sanitile** stays spotless longer.

Weather resistant wrought iron furniture is used indoors and out.

Stainless steel products for the kitchen, such as dishes and cutlery, increase in acceptance and craftsmanship.

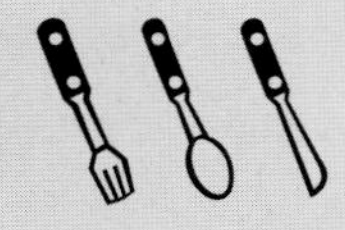

Swivel chairs and tables from the office are now prevalent at home.

Textured carpets and wallpapers help complete every room in the house.

TELEVISION'S INCREASING POPULARITY GIVES RISE TO THE NEWEST PART OF THE HOME – THE TELEVISION ROOM, COMPLETE WITH COMFORTABLE CHAIRS AND SMALL REFRESHMENT TABLES.

Modern furniture continues to outsell classic.

"FOR MODERN LIVING"
at the Detroit Institute of Arts
features over 3,000 modern design pieces from the U.S. and Europe. Furniture, fabrics and toys are among the many items on view. Featured is Charles Eames' newest chair design, "La Chaise."

"Sword In The Desert" Has A Gala Opening On Broadway

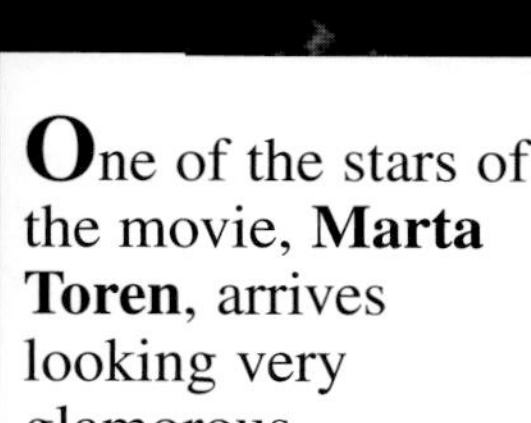

One of the stars of the movie, **Marta Toren**, arrives looking very glamorous.

Police and admiring fans strain to catch a glimpse of the beautiful Universal International star **Yvonne de Carlo**.

Miss de Carlo presents Sweden's prize to the film world, Miss Toren, a scroll from Universal Pictures.

Yes... film executives, critics and fans alike all flock to another outstanding showing of America's gift to movie lovers all over the world.

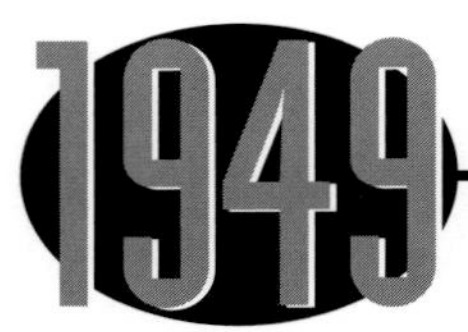

SPECIAL ACADEMY AWARD HONORS*

Fred Astaire: "For his unique artistry and his contributions to the technique of musical pictures."

Cecil B. DeMille: "For his 37 years of screen showmanship."

** Award presented at 1950 ceremony.*

International Film Festival Best Acting Award

OLIVIA DE HAVILLAND
"The Snake Pit"

JOSEPH COTTON
"Portrait Of Jennie"

Walter & **John Huston** receive Oscars for "The Treasure Of The Sierra Madre" becoming the first father and son to be so honored.

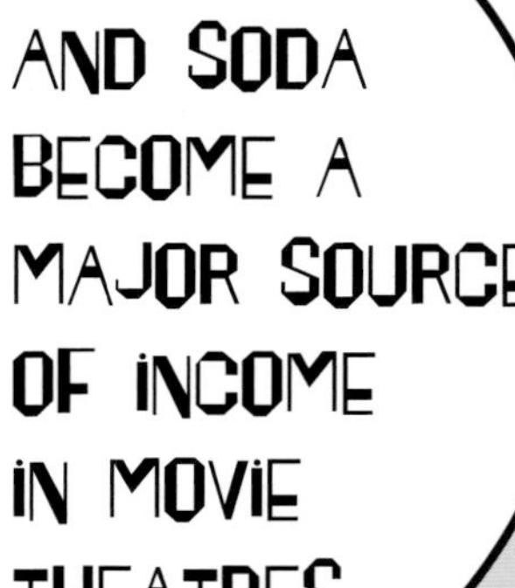

POPCORN, CANDY AND SODA BECOME A MAJOR SOURCE OF INCOME IN MOVIE THEATRES.

HIGHEST GROSSING FILM

"Jolson Sings Again"

Passings

Academy Award winner for "GONE WITH THE WIND," director **Victor Fleming**, 60, dies from a heart attack.

Star of radio, stage and screen, **Frank Morgan**, best known for his comic roles, especially the title role in "THE WIZARD OF OZ," dies at age 59.

One of Hollywood's top earners, Academy Award winning actor **Wallace Beery**, star of "THE CHAMP" and former elephant trainer, dies at age 63.

FAMOUS BIRTHS

Armand Assante
Ed Begley, Jr.
Janet Maslin
Jeff Bridges
Jessica Lange
Lawrence Kasden
Richard Gere
Save Tibet
Pam Grier
Meryl Streep
Sigourney Weaver
Sissy Spacek
Teri Garr

1949

The Academy Awards 1949 Ceremony
(For 1948 Films)

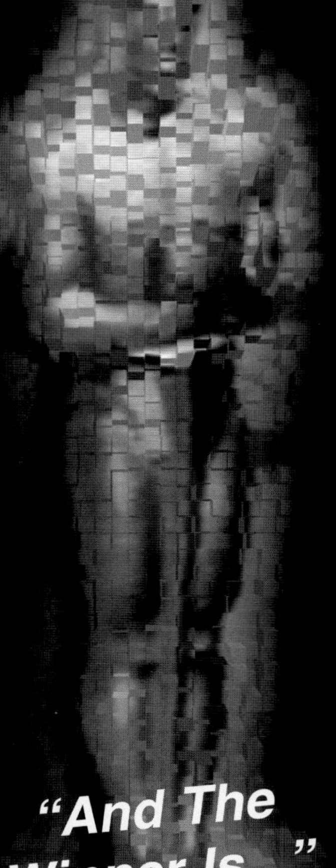

BEST PICTURE
Hamlet

BEST ACTOR
LAURENCE OLIVIER, *Hamlet*

BEST ACTRESS
JANE WYMAN, *Johnny Belinda*

BEST DIRECTOR
JOHN HUSTON,
The Treasure Of The Sierra Madre

BEST SUPPORTING ACTOR
WALTER HUSTON,
The Treasure Of The Sierra Madre

BEST SUPPORTING ACTRESS
CLAIRE TREVOR, *Key Largo*

BEST SONG
"BUTTONS AND BOWS," *The Paleface*

Laurence Olivier

1949 Favorites *(Oscars Presented In 1950)*

BEST PICTURE
All The King's Men

BEST ACTOR
BRODERICK CRAWFORD, *All The King's Men*

BEST ACTRESS
OLIVIA DE HAVILLAND, *The Heiress*

BEST DIRECTOR
JOSEPH L. MANKIEWICZ, *A Letter To Three Wives*

BEST SUPPORTING ACTOR
DEAN JAGGER, *Twelve O'Clock High*

BEST SUPPORTING ACTRESS
MERCEDES MCCAMBRIDGE, *All The King's Men*

BEST SONG
"BABY, ITS COLD OUTSIDE," *Neptune's Daughter*

FILM FAVORITES

A Connecticut Yankee In King Arthur's Court
A Letter To Three Wives
Adam's Rib
Adventures Of Don Juan
ALL THE KING'S MEN
Always Leave Them Laughing
ANNA LUCASTA
BATTLEGROUND
Calamity Jane And Sam Bass
CHAMPION
Christopher Columbus
Dancing In The Dark
East Side, West Side
FRANCIS
HAPPENS EVERY SPRING
Holiday Affair
Home Of The Brave
I WAS A MALE WAR BRIDE
In The Good Old Summertime
Intruder In The Dust
Jolson Sings Again
Kind Hearts And Coronets
LITTLE WOMEN

SAMSON and DELILAH

WHITE HEAT

the BICYCLE THIEF

LOST BOUNDARIES
Love Happy
Madame Bovary
Mr. Belvedere Goes To College
My Friend Irma
NOT WANTED
Oh, You Beautiful Doll
ON THE TOWN
Once More, My Darling
PINKY
Portrait Of Jenny
RED, HOT AND BLUE
Samson And Delilah
Sands Of Iwo Jima
She Wore A Yellow Ribbon
So Dear To My Heart
SWORD IN THE DESERT
TAKE ONE FALSE STEP
TASK FORCE
That Forsyte Woman
The Adventures Of Ichabod And Mr. Toad
The Bicycle Thief
The Big Steal
The Black Book

The Blue Lagoon
THE FOUNTAINHEAD
The Girl From Jones Beach
The Great Gatsby
The Great Lover
The Great Sinner
The Hasty Heart
THE HEIRESS
The Home Of The Brave
THE RECKLESS MOMENT
The Red Danube
The Red Menace
THE SET UP
The Story Of Seabiscuit
The Stratton Story
THE THIRD MAN
They Live By Night
THIEVES' HIGHWAY
TOKYO JOE
Top O' The Morning
Twelve O'Clock High
We Were Strangers
WHITE HEAT
YES SIR, THATS MY BABY

PINKY

Top Box Office Stars

Bob Hope
Bing Crosby
Bud Abbott &
Lou Costello
John Wayne
Gary Cooper
Betty Grable
Esther Williams
Cary Grant
Humphrey Bogart
Clark Gable

John Wayne

Barbara Bel Geddes

Rising Stars

Montgomery Clift
Kirk Douglas
Betty Garrett
Paul Douglas
Howard Duff
Pedro Armendariz
Dean Stockwell
Wanda Hendrix
Wendell Corey
Barbara Bel Geddes

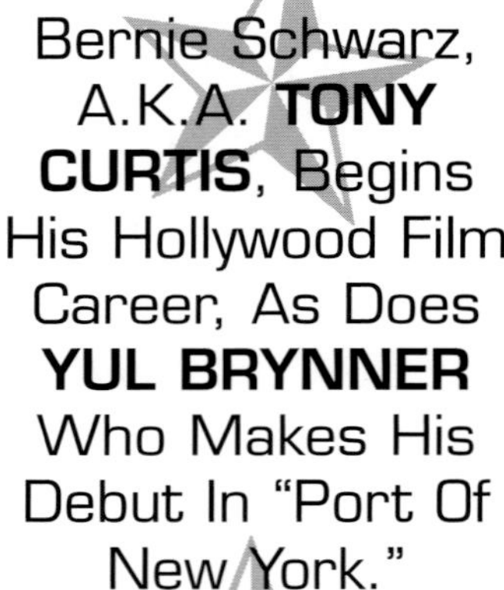

Bernie Schwarz, A.K.A. **TONY CURTIS**, Begins His Hollywood Film Career, As Does **YUL BRYNNER** Who Makes His Debut In "Port Of New York."

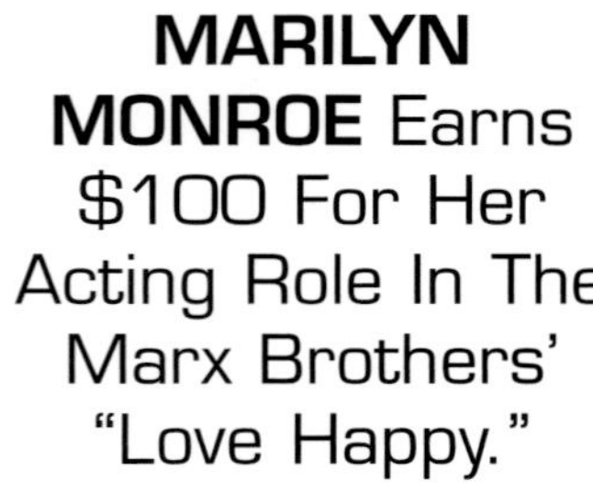

MARILYN MONROE Earns $100 For Her Acting Role In The Marx Brothers' "Love Happy."

Celebrities from all over the world converge on the South of France for the annual CANNES FILM FESTIVAL

Among some of the stars in attendance are **Eric von Stroheim** *(above)* and **Martine Carroll** *(below).*

The French Ballet provides dance relief.

American screen tough guy **Edward G. Robinson** addresses the glittering audience.

1949 ADVERTISEMENT

Why RCA Victor can give you such a BIG PICTURE at such a SMALL PRICE

Low-cost 16" picture tube was developed by RCA scientists and engineers. Using *metal* sides and a glass face cuts big-picture costs tremendously . . . yet improves picture quality!

Another saving results from RCA Victor's matchless "know-how". . . over 3 generations of experience in making precision instruments.

***The finest in service!** RCA Victor offers you *direct factory service* with the optional RCA Victor Television Owner Contract. The reasonable fee covers *all charges for ántenna, complete installation by RCA's own factory service experts and guaranteed performance.*

Have you met "Kukla, Fran and Ollie"—with Burr Tillstrom's wonderful characters? See them on your NBC television station.

A complete home entertainment unit is this magnificent Chippendale-style cabinet! Includes big, 16-inch Eye Witness television, plus powerful radio for standard, RCA Victor FM and short wave. Two record changers . . . for 78 rpm records and the wonderful new 45 rpm RCA Victor records . . . with the "Magic Monitor" that makes old records sound new. Has the exclusive "Golden Throat" tone system. AC operation. RCA Victor 9TW390.

Only $795.00†
plus $14.42 Fed. Tax
Installation extra.*

RCA Victor 9JY plays the new "45" records thru any set! It's the modern, inexpensive way to enjoy recorded music. Only $12.95.

WORLD LEADER IN RADIO . . .
FIRST IN RECORDED MUSIC . . .
FIRST IN TELEVISION

DIVISION OF RADIO CORPORATION OF AMERICA

1949

POPULAR DAYTIME RADIO SHOWS

ARTHUR GODFREY
AUNT JENNY
BIG SISTER
MA PERKINS
OUR GAL SUNDAY
PEPPER YOUNG'S FAMILY
RIGHT TO HAPPINESS
ROMANCE OF HELEN TRENT
WENDY WARREN
YOUNG WIDDER BROWN

POPULAR EVENING RADIO SHOWS

BING CROSBY
CHARLIE McCARTHY
CRIME PHOTOGRAPHER
FIBBER McGEE & MOLLY
GODFREY'S TALENT SCOUTS
JACK BENNY
MY FRIEND IRMA
RADIO THEATRE
SUSPENSE
WALTER WINCHELL

RADIO

HITTING THE AIRWAVES FOR THE FIRST TIME

DRAGNET

FATHER KNOWS BEST

Jerry Lewis

NBC's new comedy team **JERRY LEWIS** and **DEAN MARTIN** begin an NBC radio series. Network has trouble finding a sponsor.

- **GROUCHO MARX Wins Radio's Highest Honor—The Peabody Award.**

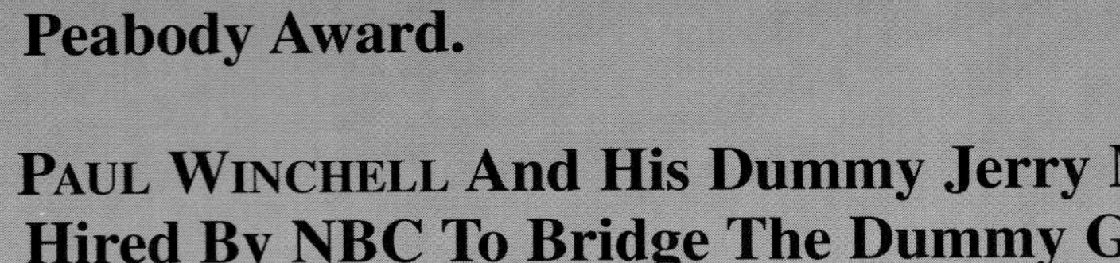

- **PAUL WINCHELL And His Dummy Jerry Mahoney Are Hired By NBC To Bridge The Dummy Gap After Edgar Bergen And Charlie McCarthy Move Over To CBS.**

- **Radio Station KOWH In Omaha Introduces The Disc Jockey Format Including Repetitive Airplay Of Selected Recordings, Chatter, News Breaks And Jingles.**

- **In An Effort To Break NBC's Domination Of The Radio Audience, Chairman Of CBS, William S. Paley, Gets Jack Benny To Move To CBS After 16-Year Run On NBC And Other NBC Stars Follow, Including Edgar Bergen, Bing Crosby And Red Skelton.**

Eddie Cantor

SIGNING OFF FOR THE LAST TIME

CAPTAIN MIDNIGHT

THE EDDIE CANTOR SHOW

KAY KYSER'S KOLLEGE OF MUSICAL KNOWLEDGE

THE KRAFT MUSIC HALL

THANKS FOR THE MEMORIES

JOE FRANKLIN Begins Broadcasting His "Joe Franklin's Memory Lane" At Radio Station WOR-AM.

1949 ADVERTISEMENT

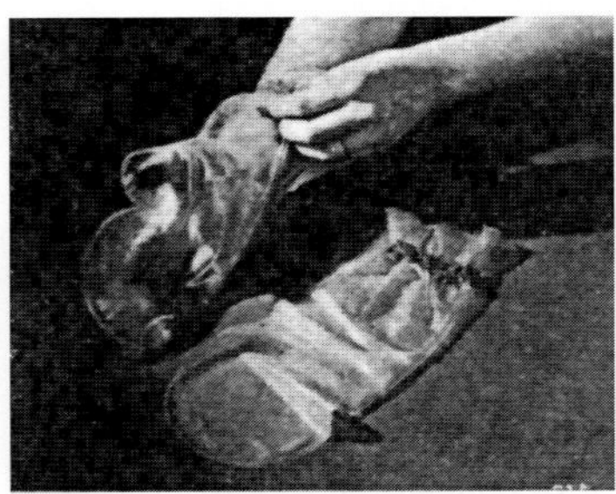

No More Dishpan Hands!

Waterproof, silky textured PLASTI-MITTS protect your hands, guard rings, watches and cuffs from splashing water. Pleasant to wear. Won't chip, crack, peel or stain.

49¢ *a pr. ppd.*

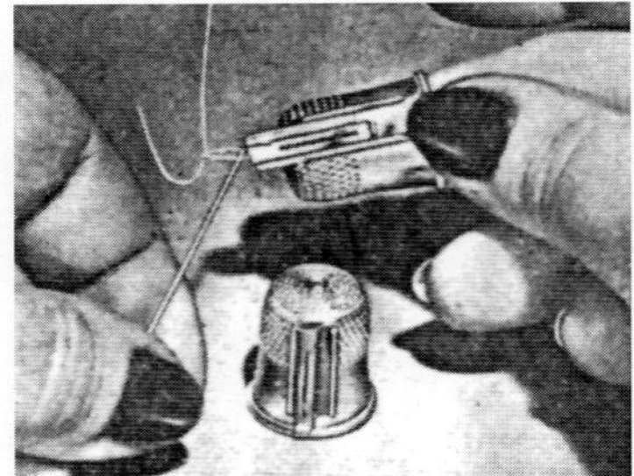

Amazing New Magic Thimble

has a built-in automatic needle threader that works simply and easily. Plus a built-in automatic thread cutter. Sizes: Med. Large & Med. Small

DELUXE MODEL—GOLD PLATED. BOXED .... **49¢** *ea. ppd.*

STANDARD MODEL—NICKEL PLATED .... **3** *for* **49¢** *ppd.*

Satisfaction Guaranteed. Send Check or M.O. No Stamps or C.O.D.'s

OUR BIG BEAUTIFUL NEW GIFT CATALOG SENT **FREE.** UNUSUAL GIFTS FROM ALL OVER THE WORLD AT REASONABLE PRICES.

Spencer Gifts OF **Atlantic City, N. J.**

1949 ADVERTISEMENT

PICTURE OF GOOD SERVICE

When you think of telephone service, we'd like you to think of friendly, competent people, genuinely eager to serve you in every way.

The Operator is an important part of the picture when she puts through your calls quickly and courteously, or renders some special service in an emergency.

The Girl in the Business Office shows the same spirit by being alert and pleasant when you pay a bill or there's something you'd like to know about the service.

The Installer helps you to think well of the Company by being polite and efficient and tidy when he comes to your home to put in a telephone.

The Company itself does its part when it conducts itself as a good citizen, as well as a good telephone organization, in the communities in which it operates.

All across the land, you will find teamwork and neighborliness among telephone people. They take satisfaction in providing a valuable service to the public.

BELL TELEPHONE SYSTEM

1949 TELEVISION

T.V. FAVORITES

The Aldrich Family
The Bigelow Show
Blind Date
Break The Bank
Candid Camera
Cavalcade Of Stars
The Cliff Edwards Show
Colgate Theatre
The Ed Sullivan Show
The Ed Wynn Show
Eddie Condon's Hour Show
Face The Music
The Front Page
Garroway At Large
Inside U.S.A.
Kukla, Fran & Ollie
Leave It To The Girls
The Life Of Riley

Kukla, Fran & Ollie

Paul Whiteman

Perry Como

Boris Karloff

Lights Out
The Milton Berle Show
The Morey Amsterdam Show
Paul Whiteman's Goodyear Revue
The Perry Como Show
Philco Television Playhouse
Ripley's Believe It Or Not
Starring Boris Karloff
Studio One
Suspense
Tex And Jinx
We, The People
The Wendy Barrie Show
Window On The World
Winner Take All

PROGRAMS MAKING THEIR T.V. DEBUT

Arthur Godfrey and his Friends
The Big Story
Captain Video and his Video Rangers
Fireside Theatre
Ford Theatre
The Fred Waring Show
The Goldbergs
Hopalong Cassidy
I Remember Mama
The Lone Ranger
Man Against Crime
Mr. Imagination
Paul Whiteman's T.V. Teen Club
Quiz Kids
Roller Derby
Stop The Music
This Is Show Business
Twenty Questions
The Voice of Firestone

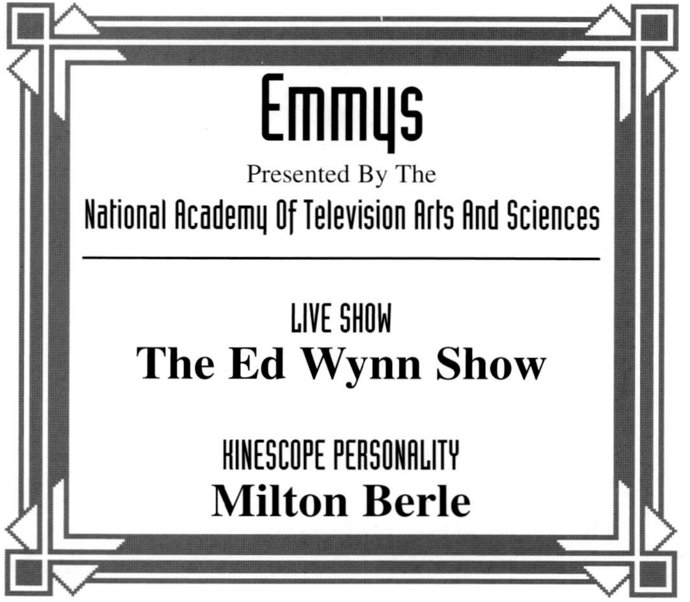

MILTON BERLE SIGNS WITH TEXACO FOR HIS SHOW AT $10,000 A WEEK, UP FROM $2,500 LAST SEASON.

MILTON BERLE DOES ONE MAN TV FUNDRAISER FOR 16 HOURS RAISING MORE THAN ONE MILLION DOLLARS FOR THE DAMON RUNYON MEMORIAL FUND.

☞ The new "Admiral Broadway Revue" starring MARGE and GOWER CHAMPION, SID CAESAR, IMOGENE COCA and MARY MCCARTY is the most expensive revue on the air with a weekly cost of $25,000.

☞ JOHN CAMERON SWAYZE hosts "The Camel News Caravan" news show "hopscotching the world for headlines" and signing off with *"That's the story, glad we could get together."*

FAMOUS BIRTHS

Brandon Tartikoff
Don Johnson
Garry Shandling
Lindsay Wagner
Michael Richards
Paul Shaffer
Shelley Long
Vicki Lawrence

U.S. Department Of Commerce Issues A Report Stating That:
Television's combination of moving pictures, sound and immediacy produces an impact that extends television as an advertising medium into the realm of personal sales solicitation.

FCC Adopts Fairness Doctrine Making Broadcasters Responsible For Presenting All Sides Of A Controversial Issue.

Linkage Begins Between The East And Mid-West For The First Time Allowing Live Network Programming To Reach One-Fourth Of The Nation's Television Viewers Kicking It Off With A Special Broadcast Including Arthur Godfrey, Ted Steele, Milton Berle and Harry Richman.

The FCC Bans Radio And Television Prize Shows But Despite A Restraining Order Against The FCC, 38 Programs Go Off The Air.

☞ Sir Laurence Olivier arrives in New York to make his television debut.

☞ Westinghouse hires Betty Furness as the official spokeswoman for its refrigerators and appliances.

☞ Time-Life produces "Crusade In Europe," the first television documentary series.

☞ Los Angeles-based "Time For Beany" is the first children's program syndicated to other stations via kinescope.

☞ The Park Sheraton Hotel is the first to place a television set in every room at no extra charge.

WOMEN'S ROLLER DERBY Makes Its Debut Which Calls On The Women To Use Just About Any Means They Want To Pass A Rival Skater.

1949 POPULAR SONGS

Again	*Gordon Jenkins*
A Dreamer's Holiday	*Perry Como*
A Little Bird Told Me	*Evelyn Knight & The Stardusters*
A Wonderful Guy	*Mary Martin*
Baby, It's Cold Outside	*Dinah Shore & Buddy Clark*
Bali Ha'i	*Perry Como*
The Blossoms On The Bough	*The Andrews Sisters*
Bluebird On Your Windowsill	*Doris Day*
Cabaret	*Rosemary Clooney*
Careless Hands	*Mel Torme*
Cruising Down The River	*Russ Morgan & The Skylarks*
Dear Hearts And Gentle People	*Bing Crosby*
Diamonds Are A Girl's Best Friend	*Carol Channing*
Do The Huckle Buck	*Frank Sinatra*
Don't Cry, Joe	*Johnny Desmond*
Far Away Places	*Bing Crosby*
Happy Talk	*Juanita Hall*
He Calls Me Crazy	*Billie Holiday*
I Can Dream, Can't I?	*Patty Andrews*
I'm So Lonesome I Could Cry	*Hank Williams*
Lady Of Spain	*Ray Noble*
Land Of Love	*Nat "King" Cole*
Let's Take An Old-Fashioned Walk	*Doris Day*
Lovesick Blues	*Hank Williams*
Mona Lisa	*Nat "King" Cole*
Mule Train	*Frankie Laine*
Once In Love With Amy	*Frank Sinatra*
Powder Your Face With Sunshine	*Buddy Clarke & Doris Day*
Riders In The Sky	*Vaughn Monroe*
Rudolph, The Red-Nosed Reindeer	*Gene Autry*
Slippin' Around	*Margaret Whiting & Jimmy Wakely*
Smokey Mountain Boogie	*Tennessee Ernie Ford*
Some Enchanted Evening	*Ezio Pinza*
That Lucky Old Sun	*Frankie Laine*
Who Do You Know In Heaven	*The Ink Spots*
You're Breaking My Heart	*Vic Damone*

Gene Autry

Nat "King" Cole

BING CROSBY

1949 ADVERTISEMENT

New Recording Artists

AMES BROTHERS

FATS DOMINO

TENNESSEE ERNIE FORD

BURL IVES

B.B. KING

DEAN MARTIN

HANK WILLIAMS

Receives five minutes of solid applause after singing his hit single **"Lovesick Blues"** at the Grand Ole Opry.

Billboard

Magazine begins using the category **Country & Western** which replaces its **Folk Tunes** category.

- The **TOP 40** Format Kicks Off At A Radio Station In Omaha.
- **Irving Berlin** Makes A Deal With Paramount For A Film Starring Bing Crosby Based On His Hit Song "White Christmas."
- Larry LaPrise Makes The First Recording Of **"The Hokey Pokey."**

The first record catalog is created by William Schwann, a record store owner in Cambridge, Massachusetts.

RCA Victor releases its first 45-rpm records.

Philco creates a turntable and arm for adapting record players so they can play the three types of available records—78's, 45's and 33 1/3's.

The "Oklahoma" LP is the first Broadway soundtrack to be sold in a boxed set.

After A Year In The Hospital Recovering From Injuries Sustained In A Car Accident, LES PAUL Electrifies Jazz Followers At Chicago's THE BLUE NOTE With his Les Paul Trio.

Jazz And Blues Singer JIMMY WITHERSPOON'S Recording Of "Ain't Nobody's Business" Tops The R&B Charts For 34 Weeks.

ROSEMARY CLOONEY Goes Solo.

BILLIE ECKSTINE Is Named Most Popular Singer By DOWNBEAT For The Second Year.

A quintet is formed by jazz musician GEORGE SHEARING.

BOP MUSIC Continues To Surge In Popularity And Is Described In Downbeat Magazine By CHARLIE PARKER As: *"It's Trying To Play Clean And Looking For The Pretty Notes."*

- Following Ezra Pound's winning of the Bollingen Prize, the Library Of Congress discontinues all prizes for art, music and literature on the recommendation of Congress.
- Pete Seeger and the Weavers perform at Manhattan's Village Vanguard.
- Guy Lombardo and his Royal Canadians celebrate 25 years as a dance band.

1949 ADVERTISEMENT

Enjoy 4 hours

CONTINUOUS RECORDED MUSIC!

Want to hear how wonderful recorded music can be—when touched by the magic of the G-E Electronic Reproducer? Hear this new G-E console, performance-engineered at Electronics Park, *for the finest record reproduction you ever heard!* It plays *both* standard and long-playing records. Enjoy a whole evening's entertainment at a single loading of the changer! Plus *both* FM and AM radio—in **natural color tone!** Exquisite cabinet veneered in genuine mahogany (Model 324-LP) or blond American oak (Model 328-LP). Hear a demonstration today!

G-E radios from $19.95*

**Prices slightly higher West and South—subject to change without notice.*

PERFORMANCE-ENGINEERED AT ELECTRONICS PARK

You can put your confidence in—

GENERAL ELECTRIC

FAMOUS BIRTHS

Alan Menken
Annie Leibovitz
Billy Joel
Bonnie Raitt
Bruce Springsteen
Lionel Richie
Maureen McGovern
John Oates
Eddie Money
Maurice Gibb
Robin Gibb
Rick Springfield
Tom Waits
Hank Williams, Jr.

Passings

Huddie Ledbetter, better known as **Leadbelly**, folk singer, master 12-string guitar player and writer of songs such as "Rock Island Line," dies at 64 from Lou Gehrig's Disease.

One of the musicians responsible for making New Orleans jazz world famous, **Willie "Bunk" Johnson**, trumpet player, band leader and jazz pioneer dies at age 69.

Decca Records president and founder **Jack Kapp**, who signed Al Jolson and Bing Crosby to recording contracts, dies at age 47.

Composer **Herbert Stothart**, whose work for "The Wizard Of Oz" garnered him an Academy Award, dies at age 64.

1949

ON BROADWAY

Arthur Miller's DEATH OF A SALESMAN is the First Play to Win All Three Top U.S. Drama Awards—New York Drama Critics' Circle, the Pulitzer and the Antoinette Perry Award.

Lee J. Cobb on the left.

Another Opening, Another Night

GENTLEMEN PREFER BLONDES

Carol Channing

SOUTH PACIFIC

Mary Martin and Myron McCormick

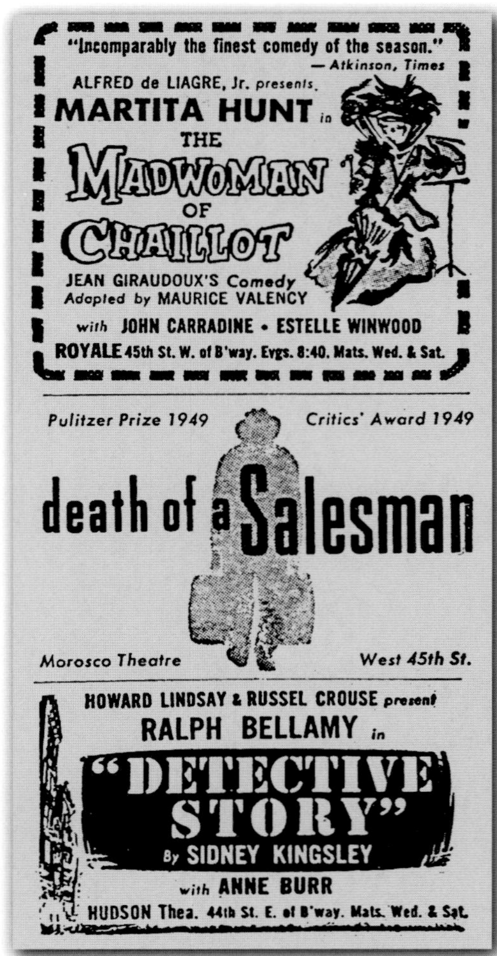

Eager to see **South Pacific** playgoers pay as much as $50 for a $6.60 ticket. Box office receipts break records with an average weekly gross of over $50,000.

Lee J. Cobb's impressive performance as Willy in **Death Of A Salesman** earns him star billing and his name goes on the marquee.

PASSINGS

Author of The Philadelphia Story, playwright **Philip Barry** dies at age 53.

On Broadway

A Streetcar Named Desire

Anne Of The Thousand Days

As The Girls Go

At War With The Army

Born Yesterday

Detective Story

Diamond Lil

Edward, My Son

Goodbye, My Fancy

High Button Shoes

Howdy Mr. Ice!

Kiss Me, Kate

Lend Me An Ear

Lost In The Stars

Miss Liberty

Mister Roberts

Monteserrat

Private Lives

Regina

Texas Li'l Darlin'

The Browning Version

The Father

The Madwoman Of Chaillot

The Silver Whistle

The Traitor

They Knew What They Wanted

Touch And Go

Where's Charley

Yes M'Lord

Pulitzer Prize for Drama

Arthur Miller
DEATH OF A SALESMAN

New York Drama Critics' Circle Award

Best Play

Arthur Miller
DEATH OF A SALESMAN

Best Foreign Play

Jean Giraudoux
THE MADWOMAN OF CHAILLOT

Best Musical

Richard Rogers & Oscar Hammerstein II
SOUTH PACIFIC

THAT LADY

Katharine Cornell *(right)* and Marian Seldes

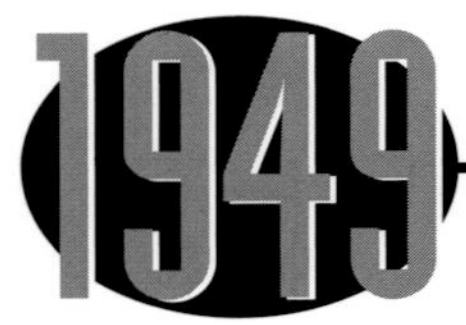

T.S. ELIOT'S Play **The Cocktail Party** Premieres In Edinburgh.

MAE WEST Returns To Broadway In The Revival Of **Diamond Lil**.

93-Year Old GEORGE BERNARD SHAW'S **Buoyant Billions**—His First New Play In A Decade—Closes After Only A Five-Week Run In London's West End.

BERTOLT BRECHT Forms **The Berliner Ensemble**.

Vaudeville Returns To New York's Palace Theatre After A 14-Year Absence.

The **Drama Desk** Is Founded To Provide A Forum For Theater Reporters, Editors And Critics To Spotlight Areas Of Concern For The Theatrical Community.

The Actual **Tony Award** Is Now An Official Medallion Instead Of The Scroll For Female Winners And Cigarette Lighter For Male Winners Formerly Presented.

Tony Awards 1949

OUTSTANDING PLAY
"DEATH OF A SALESMAN"
Arthur Miller

OUTSTANDING MUSICAL
"KISS ME KATE"
Cole Porter,
music and lyrics
Bella and Samuel Spewack,
book

OUTSTANDING DRAMATIC ACTOR
REX HARRISON
"Anne Of The Thousand Days"

OUTSTANDING DRAMATIC ACTRESS
MARTITA HUNT
"The Madwoman Of Chaillot"

OUTSTANDING MUSICAL ACTOR
RAY BOLGER
"Where's Charley?"

OUTSTANDING MUSICAL ACTRESS
NANETTE FABRAY
"Love Life"

OUTSTANDING DIRECTOR
ELIA KAZAN
"Death Of A Salesman"

Board Set Up To Research Declining Interest In Seeing Plays.

Samuel Beckett Writes "En Attendant" (Waiting For Godot).

MALE MEMBERS OF THE CAST APPEARING IN CLIFFORD ODETS' THE BIG KNIFE PERFORM IN STREET CLOTHES WHEN THIEVES STEAL EVERYONE'S COSTUME BUT THE STAR, JOHN GARFIELD.

THE THEATER GUILD CELEBRATES ITS 30TH ANNIVERSARY.

1949 ADVERTISEMENT

Reporting the whiskey
story of the year;
the story that proves

*People know a good thing
when they taste it!*

All over America... 9 out of 10 Imperial buyers have bought Imperial before... and they're buying it again!

It's good to know... IMPERIAL

is made by Hiram Walker

91 years at fine whiskey-making makes this whiskey good. 86 proof. Blended Whiskey. The straight whiskies in this product are 4 years or more old. 30% straight whiskey. 70% grain neutral spirits. Hiram Walker & Sons Inc., Peoria, Ill.

Dance

ROLAND PETIT Brings His New Company, Les Ballets de Paris, To New York In A Dance Interpretation Of Bizet's Opera, "Carmen."

The New York City Ballet Performs JEROME ROBBINS' Ballet "Guests."

JOSE LIMON Presents The Premiere Of "La Malinche" And "Corybantic."

THE GRAND BALLET DE MONTE CARLO Premieres "The Enchanted Mill" At Covent Garden.

"The Image In The Heart" Premieres At A Special Performance Of Ballets Choreographed By TODD BOLENDER.

With MARIA TALLCHIEF in the title role, GEORGE BALANCHINE choreographs a brilliant new version of Igor Stravinsky's "Firebird."

Square dancing, the fox trot and the rumba, especially the Mambo, are the favorite dances on American dance floors, while the waltz sees an upsurge in popularity.

The **Latin Samba** Is A Hot New Ballroom Dance.

More Dance Is Seen On **Television** With A Ballet Series Introducing New Works By George Balanchine, Todd Bolender, Paul Godkin And Michael Kidd And Ballet Theatre Dances "Pas de Quatre" And "La Fille Mal Gardee."

Moira Shearer dances the title role of **Cinderella** in the new Sadler's Wells production at Covent Garden, London.

1949 ADVERTISEMENT

Bell & Howell

FILMO COMPANION

FOR ONLY $77 PLUS TAX

Takes beautiful color or black-and-white movies on low-cost 8mm film. Four speeds; fast F 2.5 Filmocoted lens. Lightest in weight and easiest to load of all spool-loading 8's.

NEW FILMO REGENT PROJECTOR
Engineered to match Filmo 8mm Cameras to show your movies at their best. Better screen illumination than any other popular make of 8mm projector, regardless of lamp power! Silent, all-geardrive. $149.50. Case, $10.

Hollywood cameramen—professional movie men—have long acclaimed Bell & Howell as makers of the world's finest movie equipment—for both professional and amateur use.

Now *you* can get the same famous make so highly prized by professional cameramen, for the cost of ordinary equipment! Now you can get your greatest dollar's worth in mechanical perfection and the certainty of superb performance! So, at these modest prices, why be satisfied with less than Bell & Howell quality? Be sure to stop at your camera dealer's soon and see the Filmo Companion with its matching projector—the new Regent.

Guaranteed for Life

During life of product, any defects in workmanship or material will be remedied free (except transportation).

A PERFECT PAIR for 16mm HOME MOVIES

FILMO DIPLOMAT
400-foot film capacity. Positive all-gear drive. Reverse, power rewind. Brilliant, flicker-free, 1000-watt illumination. With F 1.6 Filmocoted lens, $273.30, including case.

FILMO AUTO LOAD
with fast, Filmocoted F 2.5 lens for clearest pictures. Five speeds, including true slow motion. Loads quickly with black-and-white or color film magazines. $160 plus tax.

Chas. G. Clarke, A. S. C., Director of Photography for "Sand," a 20th Century Fox Technicolor production, says: "My choice for personal movies is a Bell & Howell matched pair, Filmo 8mm Camera and Projector. Why? Because these instruments have the same mark of precision that I've found in all Filmo equipment ever since I owned my very first B&H professional 35mm camera in 1921." Bell & Howell Company, 7141 McCormick Road, Chicago 45, Illinois.

Since 1907 the Largest Manufacturer of Professional Motion Picture Equipment for Hollywood and the World

London's Sadler's Wells Ballet featuring "a ballerina among ballerinas," **Margot Fonteyn**, kicks off its North American tour in New York at the Metropolitan Opera House presenting "Swan Lake" and "The Sleeping Beauty." **Moira Shearer**, **Frederick Ashton**, **Robert Helpmann** and **Beryl Grey** are members of the troupe.

The Ballet Russe de Monte Carlo performs Ruth Page's "Love Song" to Franz Schubert's music, Michel Fokine's "Carnaval" and a one-act version of "Paquita" by Alexandra Danilova.

The New York City Dance Theatre holds its first season of modern dance under the auspices of the City Center of Music and Drama. **Jose Limon** and **Merce Cunningham** among the dancers.

Passings

Bill "Bojangles" Robinson, unrivaled and innovative tap dancing star of vaudeville and motion pictures, humanitarian and vanilla ice cream lover, dies at age 71.

Classical Music

Leopold Stokowski And **Dimitri Mitropoulos** Are Appointed Principal Conductors Of The New York Philharmonic.

The Detroit Symphony Cancels Its Season Beacause Its Members Refuse A Pay Cut.

Carmel, California Holds Its 12th Annual Bach Festival.

Concerts and broadcasts celebrate **Arnold Schoenberg's** 75th Birthday.

Leonard Bernstein Wins The Boston Symphony Orchestra Merit Award For His "Age Of Innocence."

New Compositions

Piano Sonata
Samuel Barber

Music For Brass Choir
Wallingford Riegger

Piano Quintet,
Duo For Violin And Cello
Walter Piston

Cello Concerto
Virgil Thomson

Scherzo Fantasque
Ernest Bloch

Symphony No. 2 For Piano And Orchestra
Leonard Bernstein

Symphony No. 6
Sergei Prokofiev

Passings

German composer **Richard Strauss**, writer of famed operas "Salome," "Der Rosenkavalier" and "Elektra," dies at age 85.

Pulitzer Prize For Music

Virgil Thomson
music from the film
"Louisiana Story"

Premieres

Symphony No. 6
William Schuman
Dallas

Kentucky Spring
Leonard Bernstein
playing
Louisville

Symphony No. 2
(The Age Of Anxiety)
Bela Bartok, viola
Boston

Sonatas And Interludes
John Cage
New York

10 Famous Conductors Agree On What Selections Should Be Part Of A Beginning Classical Record Collection

Bach	*Brandenburg Concertos*
Beethoven	*Symphony No. 3*
Brahms	*Symphony No. 1*
Brahms	*Symphony No. 4*
Debussy	*La Mer*
Mozart	*Symphony No. 40*
Strauss	*Till Eulenspiegel*
Stravinsky	*Le Sacre du Printemps*
Tchaikovsky	*Symphony No. 6*
Wagner	*Tristan Prelude*

Metropolitan Opera Divas **Elisabetta Barbato**, **Eleanor Steber**, **Erna Berger**, **Rise Stevens** and **Dorothy Kirsten** Appear In The Opening Week Productions.

Baritone **Lawrence Tibbett** Stars In "Rigoletto" In The First Opera Of The New Season Marking His Record-Setting 25th Anniversary With The Metropolitan Opera.

Norwegian Soprano **Kirsten Flagstad** Sings Triumphantly At The San Francisco Opera House Marking Her First Appearance In America In 10 Years.

Negro Composer's "Troubled Island" Premieres In New York At The City Center Of Music And Drama.

Rudolph Bing Named To Take Over As Head Of New York's Metropolitan Opera House.

The Royal Opera House Stages Its First Premiere Since The War— "The Olympians."

The Finnish Government Awards American Contralto **Marian Anderson** Their Order Of The White Rose On Her First European Tour In 11 Years.

At The MUSEUM

An extensive Georges Braque show is mounted by the Cleveland Museum of Art and the Museum of Modern Art in New York.

San Francisco's Palace of the Legion of Honor turns 25 with an exhibit of French paintings and drawings borrowed from the Louvre.

New York's Museum of Modern Art celebrates 20th anniversary with its "Modern Art In Your Life" exhibit and begins a $3 million expansion.

Vincent Van Gogh

The largest Vincent Van Gogh show ever seen in the United States opens at the Metropolitan Museum in New York then travels to the Art Institute of Chicago. Holland's Kroller-Muller Museum and Van Gogh's nephew, Vincent, contribute paintings.

A Photography Museum opens at the Rochester, New York home of the late George Eastman, photography pioneer.

Oak Ridge, Tennessee is home to the new American Museum of Atomic Energy.

Solomon R. Guggenheim leaves more than $8 million to his art foundation.

In New York, the Metropolitan Museum of Art obtains Manet's "The Guitarist," while the nearby Museum of Modern Art acquires Picasso's "Three Musicians."

Philadelphia's Museum of Art hosts the third "Sculpture International," the grandest contemporary sculpture show in the country, featuring pieces made from wood, plaster, steel and bronze. Represented artists include Henry Moore, Alexander Calder, Isamu Noguchi, Pablo Picasso and Jean Arp.

At the Los Angeles County Museum "Thirty Masterpieces of Modern French Art" features impressionists Pissarro, Seurat, Renoir and Cezanne.

Claude Monet

Without enough financing to continue operating, the Modern Institute of Art in Beverly Hills closes its doors.

At the Ceramic National, Mary Sheier and Glidden Parker both win the Richard B. Gump Prize for the Best Designed Pottery Suitable For Mass Production.

Fan Fans at the New York Antiques Fair behold a fan made by Leonardo da Vinci as well as fans owned by Catherine the Great, Queen Victoria, Martha Washington and Empress Josephine.

Under the G.I. Bill hundreds of American veterans study painting in Paris.

The first national amateur painters competition is held.

A "Man and Wife" exhibit places works by spouses such as Pablo Picasso & Francois Gilot, Jackson Pollock & Lee Krasner and Max Ernst & Dorothea Tanning near each other.

ANDY WARHOL GRADUATES FROM THE CARNEGIE INSTITUTE OF TECHNOLOGY AND HEADS TO NEW YORK

PASSINGS

Sculptor and professor ROBERT AITKEN, who designed part of the U.S. Supreme Court building, a commemorative $50 gold coin and busts of Benjamin Franklin and Thomas Jefferson, dies at age 70.

Last of the famed seven mine-owning Guggenheim brothers, SOLOMON R. GUGGENHEIM, businessman, modern art collector and philanthropist, dies at age 88.

Socially conscious Mexican artist JOSE CLEMENTE OROZCO, master of fresco and mural painting, dies at age 65.

ART AND GOD

Henri Matisse, Georges Rouault And **Fernand Leger** Create Paintings And Stained Glass Windows For The Church Of Assy, Haute-Savoie, France.

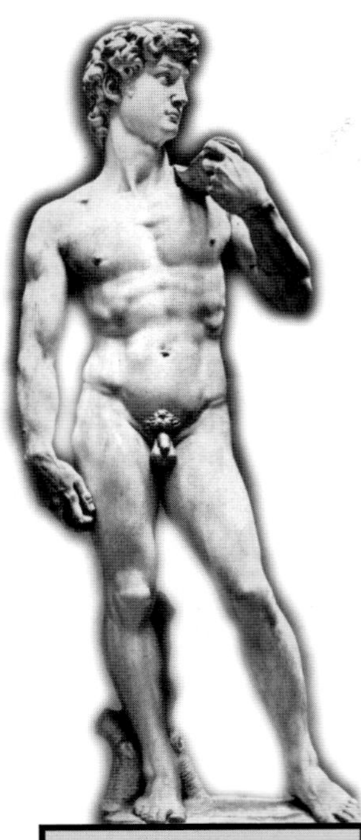

Michaelangelo's Small "David" is shown during President Truman's inauguration festivities, while the larger, more famous "David" remains in Italy. This is the first U.S. showing of any statue made by the Master.

GEORGIA O'KEEFFE is named a member of the National Institute of Arts and Letters, PABLO PICASSO an Honorary Associate.

Many PIET MONDRIAN paintings make their American debut.

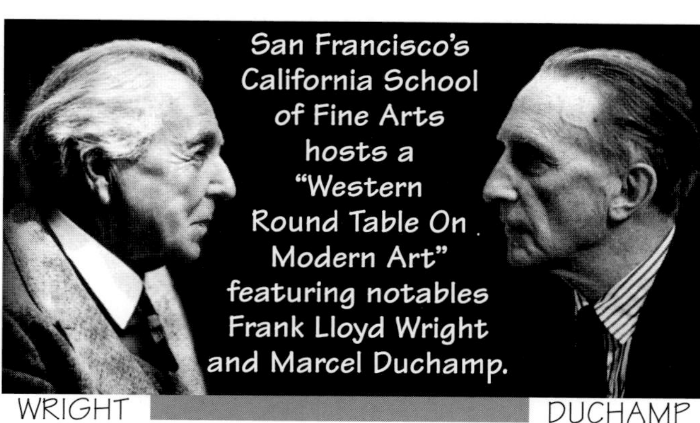

San Francisco's California School of Fine Arts hosts a "Western Round Table On Modern Art" featuring notables Frank Lloyd Wright and Marcel Duchamp.

WRIGHT DUCHAMP

Against the Hallmark Art Award, Pablo Picasso is among many signatories on an open letter stating:

"The alignment of French politics with American politics menaces our liberties too much... which aims at nothing less than the destruction of our national independence and to make the prestige of French art subservient..."

AUCTION HIGHLIGHTS

PAINTINGS

Edgar Degas	*Ballet School*	$25,000
Winslow Homer	*The Voice From The Cliffs*	$12,000
Giovanni di Paolo	*Adoration Of The Magi*	$11,000
Pierre-Auguste Renoir	*Young Bather*	$10,500
Rembrandt van Rijn	*Christ Healing The Sick*	$7,500

The painting a London woman sells for 50 shillings turns out to be Rubens' "The Suicide of Dido." It is resold for nearly $14,000.

Grandma Moses' popularity continues, and her paintings of Yankee life sell for more than $1,000.

One of five known copies of Lincoln's Gettysburg Address sells at a New York auction for $54,000.

THE PUNCH BOWL IS COMING,
THE PUNCH BOWL IS COMING

A Paul Revere-designed silver punch bowl is bought for the Boston Museum of Fine Arts. The historical piece cost $56,000, and local folks contribute much of the money.

ART PRIZES

• *The Carnegie Institute Annual* •

1st Prize	Max Beckmann	***Fisherwomen***
2nd Prize	Philip Evergood	***High Places***
3rd Prize	Hobson Pittman	***Spring Festival***

• *Pennsylvania Academy's 144th Annual* •

Temple Gold Medal	Henry Koerner	***Junk Yard***

• *National Academy's 123rd Annual* •

Altman 1st Prize	Fletcher Martin	***Cherry Tree***
Obrig Prize	Raphael Gleitsmann	***Winter Trees***

KIDZ KORNER

The American Junior Red Cross Sends Thousands Of Art Works Created By Young Americans Abroad For Viewing By Their Contemporaries In Other Countries.

Pictures By Japanese Youngsters Begin A U.S. Tour.

books

W.R. Burnett
The Asphalt Jungle

Isabel Leighton, ed.
The Aspirin Age: 1919-1941

Herb Caen
Baghdad-by-the-Bay

A. Page Cooper
The Bellevue Story

Tom Lea
The Brave Bulls

Robert Benchley
Chips Off the Old Benchley

Christopher Isherwood
The Condor and the Cows

Franz Kafka
Diaries 1914-23

Harold Robbins
The Dream Merchants

Claude Levi Strauss
The Elementary Structures of Kinship

Roy Lewis and Angus Maude
The English Middle Classes

Grace Tully
F.D.R. - My Boss

Edward Streeter
Father of the Bride

Joyce Cary
A Fearful Joy

Andre Gide

Serge Eisenstein
Film Form

James A. Michener
The Fires of Spring

J.D. Bernal
The Freedom of Necessity

Andre Gide
The Fruits of the Earth

Frank Lloyd Wright
Genius and the Mobocracy

Sinclair Lewis
The God-Seeker

Nicol Smith
Golden Doorway to Tibet

Margaret Bourke-White
Halfway to Freedom

Alexander Foote
Handbook For Spies

Albert Schweitzer
Hospital in the Jungle

Bertrand Russell
Human Knowledge: Its Scope and Limits

Arthur Koestler
Insight and Outlook

H.E. Bates
The Jacaranda Tree

Pearl S. Buck
Kinfolk

William Faulkner
Knight's Gambit

Mark Twain

Gertrude Stein; Carl van Vechten, ed.
Last Operas and Plays

Oksana Kasenkina
Leap To Freedom

Nancy Mitford
Love in a Cold Climate

Dixon Wecter, ed.
The Love Letters of Mark Twain

Hermann Hesse
Magister Ludi

Margaret Mead
Male and Female - A Study of the Sexes in a Changing World

Erich Fromm
Man For Himself

Maurice Chevalier
The Man in the Straw Hat

Nelson Algren
The Man with the Golden Arm

Judson T. Landis & Mary G. Landis
The Marriage Handbook

Famous Birth

Martin Amis

Nelson Doubleday, 59, joined the family book business, eventually becoming chairman of Doubleday & Company. Under his guidance the company grew to include book clubs, mail-order companies and bookstores throughout the country. Older brother Russell, 77, head of the firm's editorial department, dies six months later.

Former Navy man **Thomas Orlo Heggen**, author of the book Mister Roberts, and co-author of the play of the same name, drowns in his New York bathroom at age 29.

One of the founders of Poetry magazine, **Alice Corbin Henderson** dies at the age of 68.

Pulitzer Prize winning author of the popular novel Gone With The Wind, **Margaret Mitchell**, 49, dies from injuries sustained after being hit by a car in Atlanta, Georgia.

Creator of Ripley's Believe It Or Not, cartoonist, author and radio show host **Robert Ripley**, dies at age 55.

Francis Steegmuller
MAUPASSANT: A LION IN THE PATH

Winston S. Churchill
MAXIMS AND REFLECTIONS

H.L. Mencken
A MENCKEN CHRESTOMATHY

Mark van Doren
NATHANIEL HAWTHORNE

George Orwell
NINETEEN EIGHTY-FOUR

Graham Green
NINETEEN STORIES

Mary McCarthy
THE OASIS

Upton Sinclair
O SHEPHERD, SPEAK!

Willa Cather
ON WRITING

Paul Bowles

Langston Hughes
ONE-WAY TICKET

Arthur M. Schlesinger, Jr.
PATHS TO THE PRESENT

Erskine Caldwell
PLACE CALLED ESTHERVILLE

John P. Marquand
POINT OF NO RETURN

Elizabeth Janeway
THE QUESTION OF GREGORY

John O'Hara
A RAGE TO LIVE

Charles Morgan
THE RIVER LINE

Max Planck
SCIENTIFIC AUTOBIOGRAPHY AND OTHER PAPERS

Simone de Beauvoir
THE SECOND SEX

W. Somerset Maugham

Paul Tillich
THE SHAKING OF THE FOUNDATION

Paul Bowles
THE SHELTERING SKY

Elmer Rice
THE SHOW MUST GO ON

Bernard Shaw
SIXTEEN SELF SKETCHES

Graham Greene
THE THIRD MAN

Winston S. Churchill
THEIR FINEST HOUR

Eleanor Roosevelt
THIS I CAN REMEMBER

Chaim Weizmann
TRIAL AND ERROR: THE AUTOBIOGRAPHY OF CHAIM WEIZMANN

Truman Capote
A TREE OF NIGHT AND OTHER STORIES

John Erskine
VENUS, THE LONELY GODDESS

Arthur M. Schlesinger, Jr.
THE VITAL CENTER

A.B. Guthrie
THE WAY WEST

Jean-Paul Sartre
WHAT IS LITERATURE?

Billie Burke
WITH A FEATHER ON MY NOSE

Agnes Rogers
WOMEN ARE HERE TO STAY

W. Somerset Maugham
A WRITER'S NOTEBOOK

POETRY

Robert Frost
COMPLETE POEMS OF ROBERT FROST 1949

Nelly Sachs
STERNVERDUNKLUNG

Edith Sitwell
THE CANTICLE OF THE ROSE

William Carlos Williams
SELECTED POEMS

PRIZES

NOBEL

Literature:

WILLIAM FAULKNER

PULITZER

Fiction:

JAMES GOULD COZZENS
Guard of Honor

Poetry:

PETER VIERECK
Terror and Decorum

History:

ROY FRANKLIN NICHOLS
The Disruption of American Democracy

Journalism:

NEBRASKA STATE JOURNAL

Local Reporting:

MALCOLM JOHNSON
New York Sun

International Reporting:

PRICE DAY
Baltimore Sun

Editorial Cartooning:

LUTE PEASE
Newark Evening News

Biography or Autobiography:

ROBERT E. SHERWOOD
Roosevelt and Hopkins

books

Books with spiritual themes once again climb up the best-seller lists.

According to a recent survey of people who read books, 57% rent them, 31% buy them.

The Bollingen Prize goes to EZRA POUND for The Pisan Cantos, causing controversy in the literary world due to Pound's current indictment for treason and the fact he is now living in a mental institution.

The American Academy of Arts and Letters grants THOMAS MANN the Award of Merit medal and $1,000.

The New York Public Library receives the Olive Branch Petition, written by Americans to King George III around the time of the American Revolution.

Mark Twain's personal papers are to be given to the University of California.

American Authors Most Likely To Achieve Immortality

according to a poll of New Colophon subscribers

Eugene O'Neill
Sinclair Lewis
Robert Frost
Ernest Hemingway
Carl Sandburg
John Steinbeck
T.S. Eliot
H.L. Mencken
George Santayana
Edna St. Vincent Millay

The ANTIQUARIAN BOOKSELLERS ASSOCIATION of AMERICA is founded.

ROBERT E. SHERWOOD is elected to the American Academy of Arts and Letters.

The BOOK-OF-THE-MONTH CLUB sells its 100,000,000th book.

LIMITED EDITIONS CLUB GOLD MEDAL
Complete Poems of Robert Frost
Robert Frost

O. HENRY MEMORIAL AWARD
1st Prize
A Courtship
William Faulkner

DISASTERS

AN EARTHQUAKE STRIKES IN ECUADOR and in a matter of minutes villages, homes and churches are demolished.

4,000 die while survivors face suffering and heartache.

NATURE WREAKS HAVOC

on America's western plains where the worst blizzards in history pile a mantle of white death over the land.

The loss in livestock is staggering.

Operation "haylift" is begun and food is dropped out of planes to feed the cattle.

Stranded, starving cattle try to make their way to the snow-covered piles of hay.

In the most costly accident in the history of American commercial aviation, 55 are killed when a P-38 fighter plane being testflown by a Bolivian pilot, rams an Eastern Airlines DC-4 ship as it prepares to land in Washington scattering wreckage of both planes in the Potomac.

13 well-known newspapermen—including Pulitzer Prize winner Red Knickerbocker of radio station WOR—are among the 45 people killed when a Dutch transport plane crashes near Bombay, India.

Several thousand fishermen die as a typhoon sweeps the east coast of Korea hitting their fishing fleet.

120 people lose their lives when a fire destroys the Great Lakes Canadian pleasure cruiser "Noronic" at its Lake Ontario pier in Toronto.

57 Japanese are killed in Nadachi, Japan when a wartime mine drifts ashore and explodes.

9 students die in a dormitory fire at Kenyon College in Gambier, Ohio with a property loss estimated at $1,000,000.

A 300-ft. section of New York's Holland Tunnel is damaged, 23 trucks are destroyed or damaged and 60 people are injured following an explosion and fire of volatile carbon disulfide being transported in contravention of regulations aboard a 16-ton truck.

1,700 people are killed, another 100,000 left homeless and 10,000 buildings damaged or destroyed in an 18-hour fire in Chungking, China.

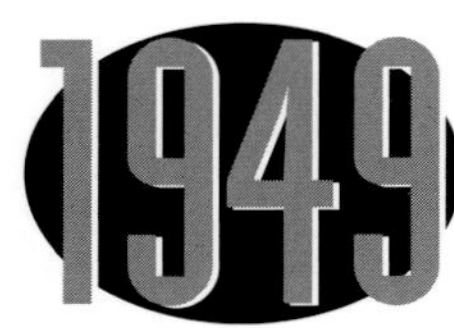

- 20 people are killed as a mob of terrified radio listeners in Quito, Ecuador attack and burn the building housing the radio station following a broadcast of H.G. Wells' War of the Worlds.
- Rain finally falls after a record-breaking 41-day drought in northeastern U.S.
- In the worst Yangtze River floods since 1931, the Chinese Nationalist news agency reports 17,000 people drown and 20,000,000 are homeless in central China.
- 10 newborn babies, two nurses and two nuns are among the 74 dead or missing in a fire which sweeps through St. Anthony's Hospital in Effingham, Illinois.
- The French government proclaims a national day of mourning after heavy rains finally put out a fire south of Bordeaux which destroys 125,000 acres of pine forests and kills 82 people including fire fighters and troops.
- In the worst earthquake ever recorded in the Pacific Northwest, a magnitude 8 temblor followed by tidal waves rocks the state of Washington causing $25,000,000 in damages, the heaviest of which is centered in the Seattle, Tacoma and Olympia areas.
- The United States rushes Red Cross workers to Guatemala following the worst floods in the country's history which wipes out 50 small communities and destroys their entire coffee crop.

THE TACOMA NARROWS BRIDGE

swings and sways during a severe storm and finally collapses into the water below.

Fashion

A TALE OF TWO CITIES

PARIS
Slender Skirts, Pockets, Low Necklines, Panels, Checks, Burlap, Taffeta Coats, Cummerbunds, Yellow, Dior's First Low-Heeled Daytime Shoes.

NEW YORK
Polka Dots, Sailor Hats, Cardigans, Carousel Silhouettes, Iridescent Cottons, Saucer Collars, Basketweave Coats, Hattie Carnegie's Bejeweled Caps, Wool Alpaca Dresses, Enka Rayon.

COTY AMERICAN FASHION CRITICS' AWARD
(The "Winnie")
Pauline Trigére

FAMOUS BIRTH *Twiggy*

Glitter and Glamour add a touch of Paris in little old New York — or... let them eat diamonds.

Napoleon and his second wife, Empress Marie-Louise, are central figures in a little drama called "Paris in New York."

Fashionable frocks by Tailored Woman along with diamonds by Van Cleef & Arpels are worth a king's ransom – or in this case, an emperor's.

"The Empress" enjoys the fashion show wearing a priceless diamond tiara and necklace.

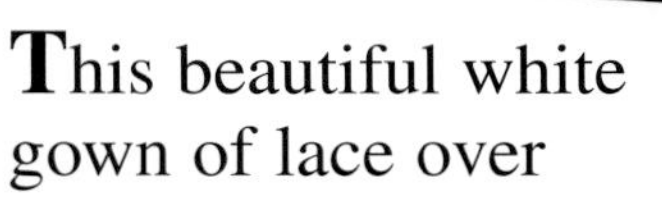

This beautiful white gown of lace over chiffon is adorned with a necklace, earclips and bracelet valued at $285,000.

This member of the Royal Court wears a green satin gown set off by spectacular diamond earrings and necklace, and agrees that diamonds are a girl's best friend.

How To Be A Well-Dressed

Undergarments

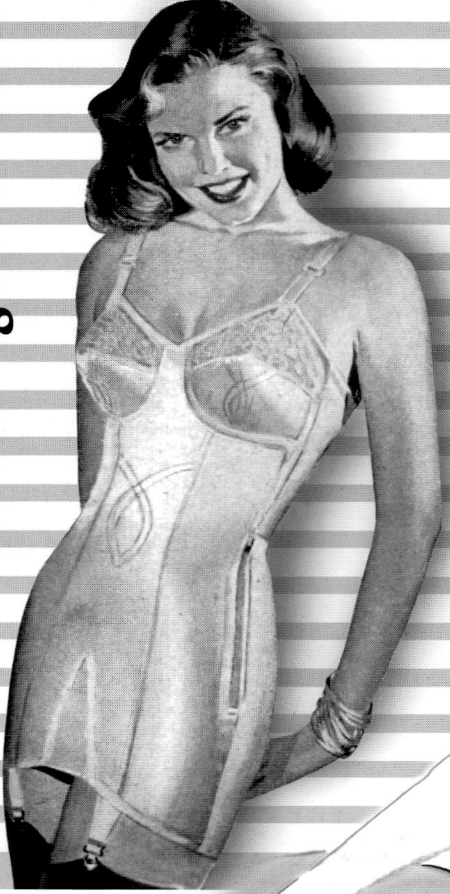

Day Wear

Try a narrow coat, short cape or bolero jacket worn over a chiffon dress, slim suit or shirtwaist dress.

Another day try a narrow skirt with pleated & peplum panels topped with an overblouse, perhaps the most important fashion item of the year, finished off with chambray shoes.

Control your body with an effective yet comfortable bone-free girdle. A silk petticoat is an asset with today's form-fitting clothes, as is a combination brassiere and camisole.

Woman Around The Clock

Afternoon Wear

As summer afternoons come and the mercury falls, a cardigan over your day outfit or your late-day colorful taffeta dress keeps you looking pretty and warm at the same time.

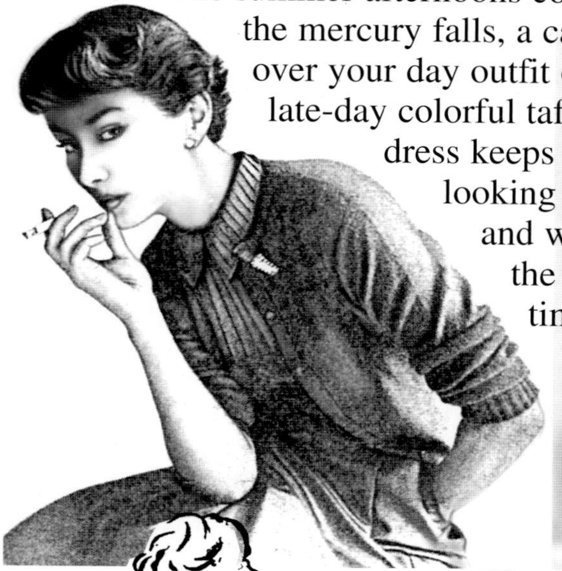

For fancier feet try surah shoes.

Evening Wear

Evening dresses can be the same length as daytime or traditional floor length.

FASHION BRIEFS

A simple pin, a thick belt and a colorful handkerchief spruce up your sweater worn over a dress, skirt or blue denim slacks. Other individual items of note include wrist-length chamois gloves or the new long gloves, silk belts, dolman sleeves and shantung purses.

A Bride In '49

Is Looking Fine In A Silk Wedding Dress With A Boned And Embroidered Bodice, Beaded Sleeves, Floor-Length Skirt And Soft Crown.

Colors Are Mixed And Matched In Bold And Creative Combinations. Feel Free To Wear Any Combination Of Beige, Green, Tangerine, Pink, Scarlet, Yellow And Navy.

The top names in French fashion travel to New York as their lower priced lines grow popular with the American consumer.

Clothing Rationing Ends In Great Britain.

Matelasse & Dobby Textures Add A Touch Of Glamour To All Materials.

A TAD OF PLAID TO DRIVE MEN MAD

1949

Chiffon, Organdy, Voile, Shantung and Marquisette Are Fabrics Good For Day Or Night.

VOGUE

Makes It Possible For Everyone To Have A Designer Dress When Their New Paris Original Patterns Go On Sale.

Ellen Tracy, Inc. Begins Designing Women's Sportswear.

UP, UP & AWAY

Skirt Lengths Are 14 Inches From The Floor – And Rising.

1949

The Shirtwaist Dress Remains A Staple In Most Women's Closets.

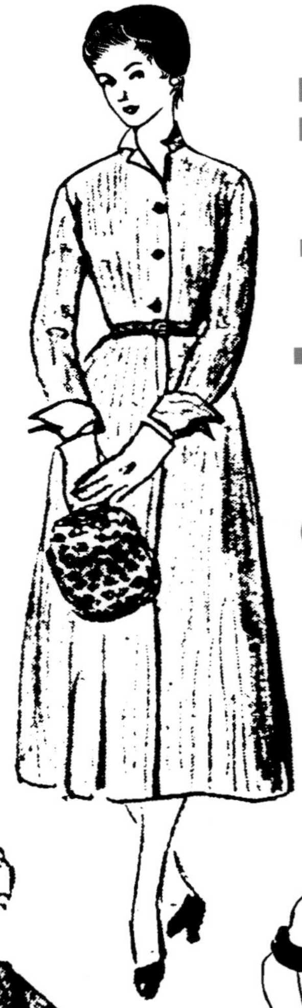

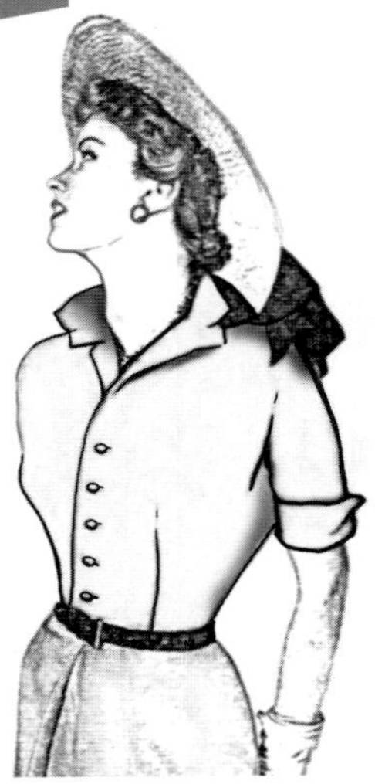

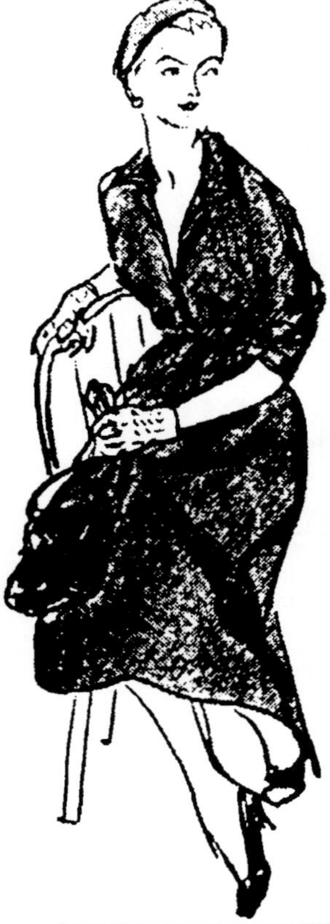

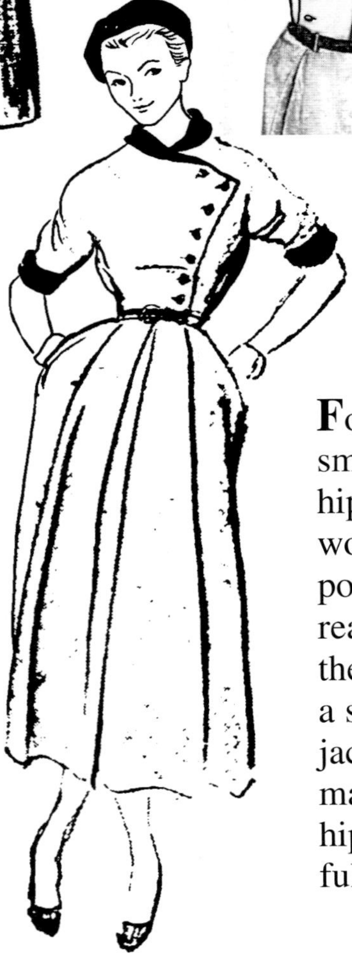

For the small hipped woman, pockets reaching the back of a suit jacket can make the hips look fuller.

1949 ADVERTISEMENT

If Mom would choose she'd choose a

Rite-Fit

a Mother's Day gift she'll cherish

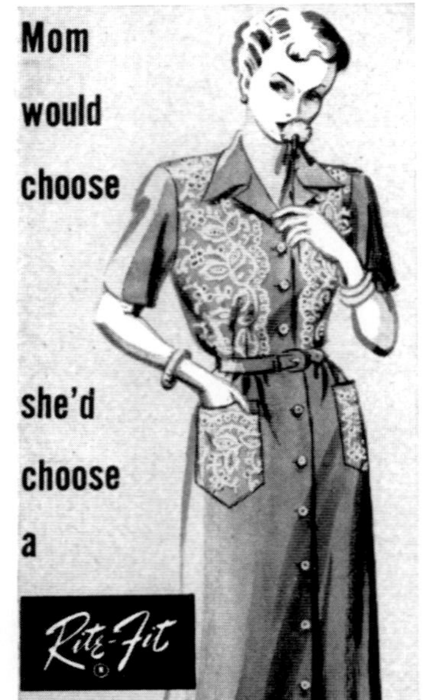

about **$8**

FEATHER FROSTING Fine quality butcher linen-weave rayon. White embroidery on Rose, Blue, Aqua, Lilac, Grey. Sizes 16½ to 24½.

These dresses are the choice of the Official Mother's Day Committee

If she's 5' 5½" or under cut costly alterations by giving a Rite-Fit half size.
14½ fits 16
16½ fits 18 & 36.
18½ fits 20 & 38
20½ fits 40
22½ fits 42
24½ fits 44

SUGAR STRIPE Printed Stripe Rayon Faille. White on Rose, Blue, Aqua, Lilac, Grey. Sizes 14½ to 24½

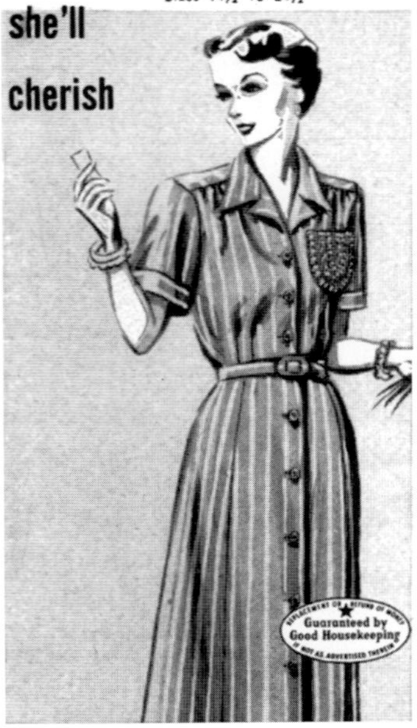

Guaranteed by Good Housekeeping

At fine stores everywhere.
For the store in your vicinity write
MAX WIESEN & SONS CO., INC.
463 Seventh Ave., New York 18, N. Y.
Mail orders filled.

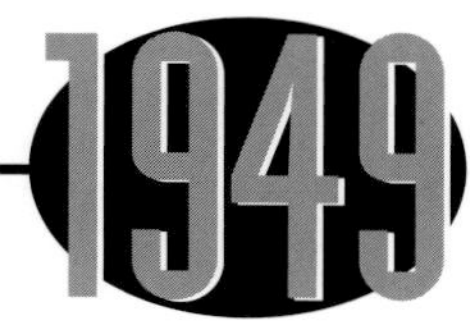

polka dots

polka dots

The National Life Conservation Society Crusades For "Birdless Hats," To Prevent The Killing Of Birds For Vanity. The Beret, Tricorn, Cloche, Turban, Slip-Cover And Pillbox Are Some Bird-Friendly Hats To Choose From.

Reminiscent Of The 1920's, The Heavily Made Up Doe-Eyed Look Returns.

The Jockey Cap Makes Its Way From The Race Track To The Cat Walk.

1949

It's in the bag

This patent leather bag is one of the latest in travel and resort bags popular this summer.

The hat of hibiscus flowers is set off by a lovely white cowhide bag accented in brown.

This trio of mermaids gather around the beach boy wearing the latest in fishnet handbags.

A beautiful brocade mandarin dress is enhanced by a matching flower-top bag.

Butterflies and flowers accent this bag perfect for cool, summery evenings.

Sugar cane tassels decorate this bucket bag – a perfect accessory for the colorful summer cotton dress.

Demonstration of drawing power.

Pineapples are the accent of the day as they adorn the dress, hat and bag.

Zippered Boots
Ankle Boots
Bicycle Shoes
Denim Shoes
Court Shoes With Peep Toes
Slingback Sandals

Over 200 Million Women's Shoes Are Manufactured In The U.S.

hey THAT LOOKS FAMILIAR

Mothers & Daughters Match Outfits While Boyfriends & Girlfriends Match Sweaters.

derful

- Opera Pumps
- Louis Heeled Opera Pumps
- Raffia Pumps
- Oxford Shoes
- Country Shoes

Rolled-Up Jeans And Ballet Shoes Are Favored By Adolescent Girls.

BROOKS BROTHERS

Classic Men's Pink Button-Down Shirt Is Such A Hit With College Girls That The Store Decides To Make One For Women.

For A Flawless Foot Finish, Use Stockings Without Visible Heel Support.

1949 ADVERTISEMENT

Here's why more than 2 million women a month choose Toni Home Permanent!

A Toni wave looks more natural! The minute you see your Toni wave in the mirror you'll see why women like Toni better than any other cold wave. Those lovely deep Toni waves are so flattering, those lustrous Toni curls look so natural!

A Toni wave is softer, easier to manage! Because the famous Toni Waving Lotion isn't harsh like hurry-up salon type solutions. Toni is a creme cold wave made definitely milder and gentler. That's why it leaves your hair in such wonderful condition —so shiny soft and natural-looking!

A Toni wave is guaranteed to last for months! A Toni wave lasts till your hair grows out and is trimmed off. What's more, a Toni is guaranteed to look every bit as lovely as the most expensive beauty salon permanent—or your money back! No wonder more women use Toni than all other cold waves combined!

It's the world's most popular permanent! Toni has given millions of perfect permanents—including every type of hair that takes a permanent, even gray, dyed, bleached or baby-fine hair. Yet the Toni DeLuxe Kit with re-usable plastic curlers costs only $2 . . . the Toni Refill only $1.

Which twin has the Toni? Lovely lustrous hair is especially important to these pretty Leigh twins because they're New York fashion models! Janet, on the right, has the Toni! She says: "I've never before had a permanent that looked so soft and natural!" And Jane says: "Next time I'm going to have the wave with the natural look, too!"

Guaranteed by Good Housekeeping

Toni HOME PERMANENT

CREME COLD WAVE

REFILL KIT Toni HOME PERMANENT

The wave that gives that natural look . . . Toni

Hair-Do's

Your hair can be molded into different shapes, depending on your mood and social obligations. The pageboy, with bangs & pin curls, is the perfect complement to a casual afternoon outfit while the chignon and french twist are the perfect styles for an evening soiree. The new gamine, short and tapered, helps create a youthful appearance.

Pearls, Crystal Baubles, Rhinestones Or Clip-On Earrings Decorate Any Outfit.

Tennis Great Gussie Moran Stuns The Audience At Wimbledon With Her Lace-Trimmed Panties That Match Her Short, Body-Hugging Dress.

Teachers Are Taught To Wear Bright Colored Garments Since Tests Have Proven Children Enjoy Having Their Instructors Wear Vivid Hues.

1949 ADVERTISEMENTS

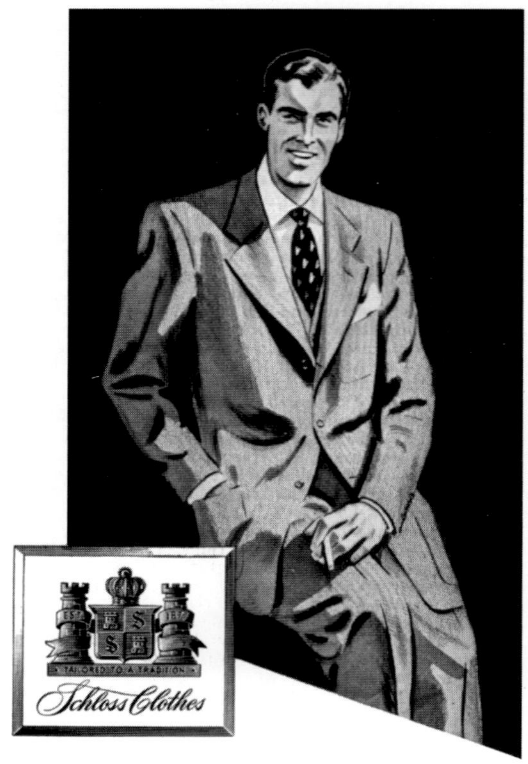

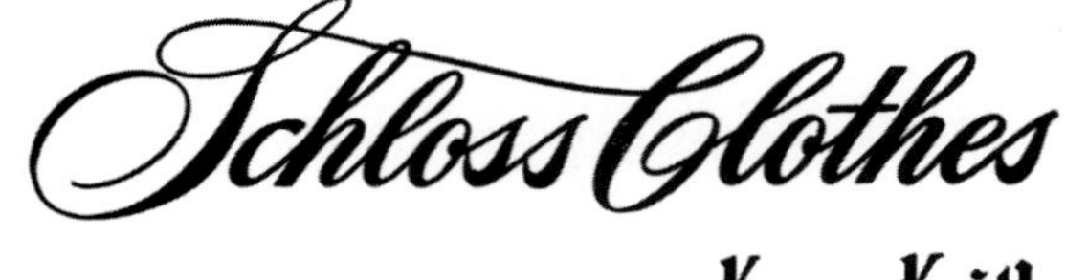

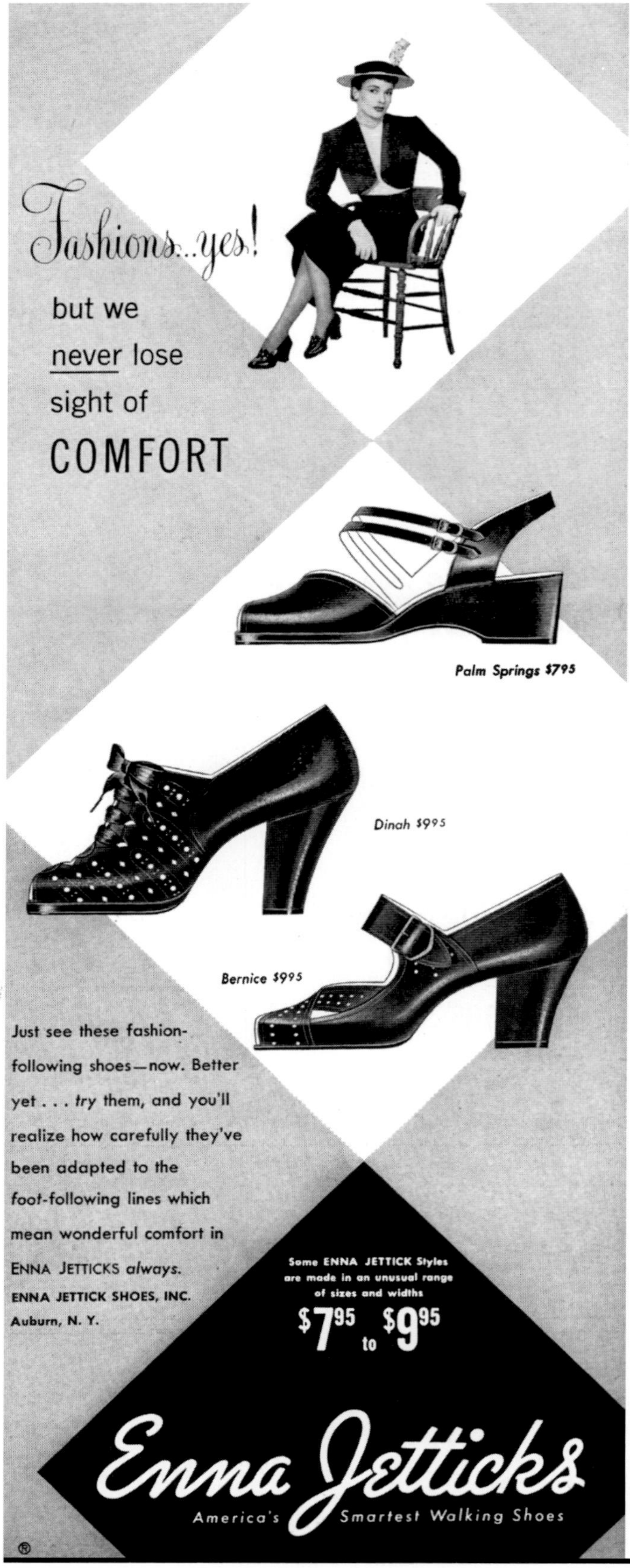
Fashions...yes!
but we never lose sight of COMFORT
Palm Springs $7.95
Dinah $9.95
Bernice $9.95
Just see these fashion-following shoes—now. Better yet . . . try them, and you'll realize how carefully they've been adapted to the foot-following lines which mean wonderful comfort in ENNA JETTICKS always.
ENNA JETTICK SHOES, INC.
Auburn, N. Y.
Some ENNA JETTICK Styles are made in an unusual range of sizes and widths
$7.95 to $9.95
Enna Jetticks
America's Smartest Walking Shoes

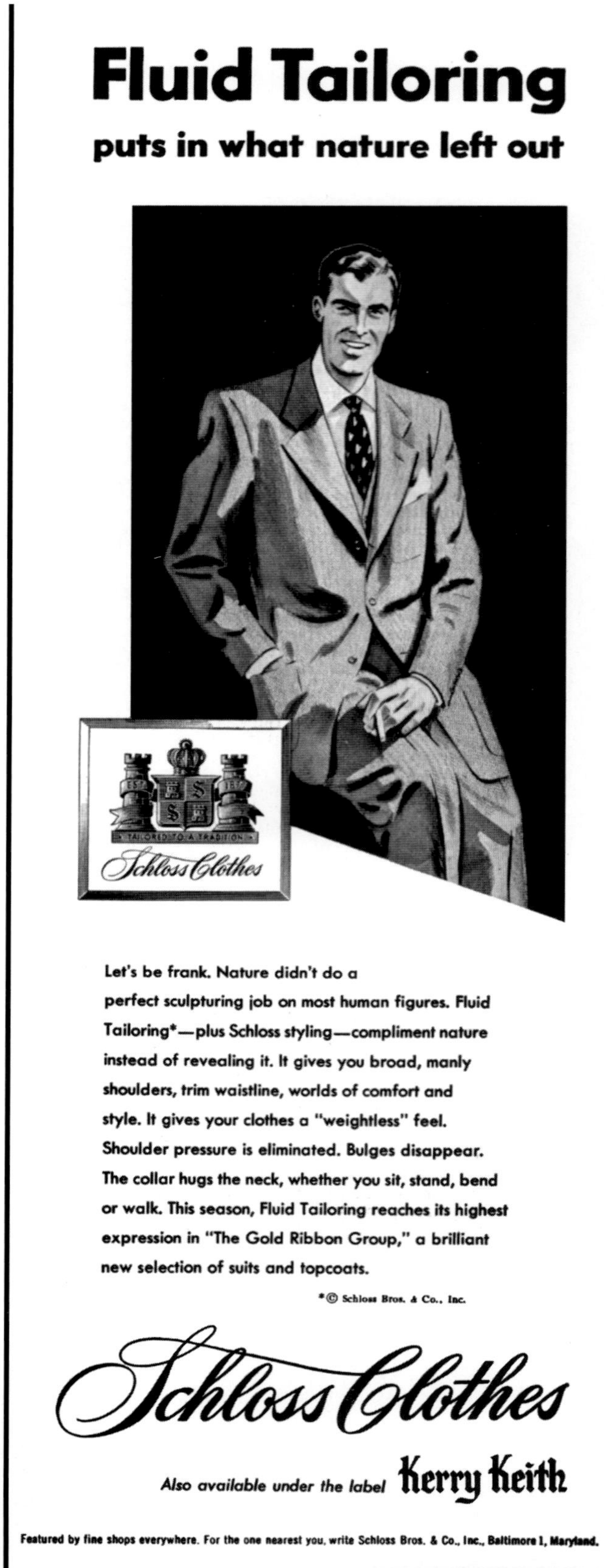
Fluid Tailoring
puts in what nature left out
TAILORED TO A TRADITION
Schloss Clothes
Let's be frank. Nature didn't do a perfect sculpturing job on most human figures. Fluid Tailoring*—plus Schloss styling—compliment nature instead of revealing it. It gives you broad, manly shoulders, trim waistline, worlds of comfort and style. It gives your clothes a "weightless" feel. Shoulder pressure is eliminated. Bulges disappear. The collar hugs the neck, whether you sit, stand, bend or walk. This season, Fluid Tailoring reaches its highest expression in "The Gold Ribbon Group," a brilliant new selection of suits and topcoats.
*© Schloss Bros. & Co., Inc.
Schloss Clothes
Also available under the label Kerry Keith
Featured by fine shops everywhere. For the one nearest you, write Schloss Bros. & Co., Inc., Baltimore 1, Maryland.

1949 Men's Fashions

FILENE'S IN BOSTON REDUCES MEN'S SUITS TO $11 AND SELLS THOUSANDS IN LESS THAN AN HOUR.

***Fred Astaire, Dean Acheson and Edward Stettinius** are a few of the best-dressed men in America.*

Fashionable hats to wear to a basketball game or the office include the snap brim, Homburg, sports and rolled brim.

When purchasing a Glen Plaid suit, make sure the plaids are even at the seams, as this is a mark of superior workmanship. A solid shirt in cream, gray, blue, tan or wine finish off the outfit nicely.

For The Summer

Cotton Neckties

Cotton T-Shirts

A Straw Hat

Madras Shirts

Summer wear influenced by university students includes madras cummerbunds and white dinner jackets with a black tie.

Try a washable suit of cotton panama cloth or the new light-weight wrinkle-free rayon-cotton blend. Another choice – a lightly lined tropical worsted.

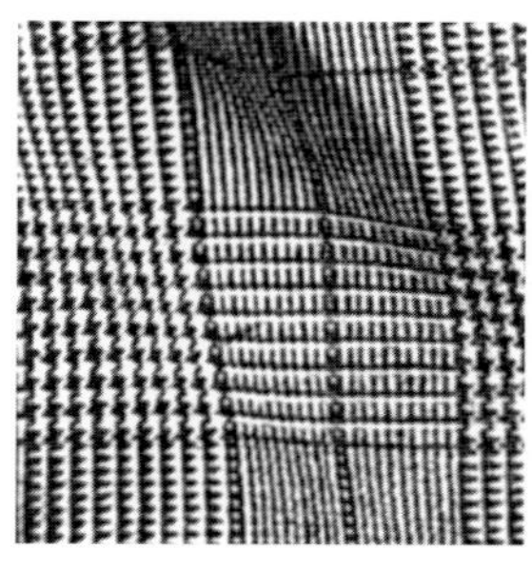

The blue double breasted Guards Coat, not seen since before the war, is worn over worsted suits in sharkskin, windowpane and nail-head patterns.

1949

You Can't Go Wrong With Dots & Checks & Fashionable Specks.

To be a truly well-dressed man, caution must be taken to match accessories with the suit. Conflicting patterns scream chaos, whereas a well thought out blend of colors and materials make a strong, confident statement. A striped suit, for example, should not be worn with a striped shirt and tie, but would go well with a solid shirt with a delicate-patterned tie. Socks can match a color in your tie, or even your shirt.

HAIR RAISING SPLENDOR

Dallas Schoolboys Favor Boogie, Bur And Hollywood Haircuts Under Colorful Caps

From Palm Beach, Red Slacks With Plaid Shirts.

1949 ADVERTISEMENT

FOR BUSINESS OR PLEASURE... *DAY OR NIGHT*

RENT A NEW CAR FROM HERTZ and Drive it yourself

AT HOME OR AWAY

Here's the happy solution to that family car problem! Here's what to do at home or away when you need a car quickly for business or pleasure! Simply rent it from Hertz as thousands of folks do, for an hour, a day, or a week, just as long as you want it. It makes no difference *where* you want to go, or *when*, there's always a big new Chevrolet or other fine car for you at your nearest Hertz station. Rates are reasonable . . . proper insurance is furnished . . . and several can ride for the same cost as one! For further information, call your local Hertz station listed under "H"—"Hertz Driv-Ur-Self"—in your telephone directory. For a complete list of all Hertz stations, and full information, write Hertz Driv-Ur-Self System, Inc., Dept. 1109, 218 South Wabash Avenue, Chicago 4, Illinois.

CHECK THESE ADVANTAGES YOU'LL ENJOY

✓ **CONVENIENT WHEREVER YOU ARE**... You can enjoy Hertz Driv-Ur-Self service—reliable, uniform, courteous—at home or in any of more than 400 cities throughout the United States, Hawaii, Cuba, Puerto Rico and Canada. Hertz is the only nation-wide and international system—largest in the world—over 25 years' experience.

✓ **PRIVATE CAR PLEASURE**... You drive a new Chevrolet or other fine car in splendid condition, properly insured, and as private as your own. Fleets have been increased over 50 per cent.

✓ **EASY AS A. B. C.**... (A) Go to a Hertz station. (B) Show your driver's license and identify yourself. (C) Step into the car and go!

✓ **RESERVATIONS**... You can reserve a car for use at home, or if traveling, before you leave home at your local Hertz station or railroad or air line ticket counters and at travel agencies. It will be ready for you on arrival.

✓ **HERTZ NATIONAL COURTESY CARDS**... As a responsible Hertz patron you are entitled to the famous Hertz National Courtesy Card. Your Courtesy Card identifies you and is honored by all Hertz stations everywhere.

✓ **INSURANCE PROTECTION** . . . Whenever you rent a car from any Hertz station you are always assured proper Public Liability, Property Damage, Fire and Theft Insurance—written with reliable companies.

✓ **A TYPICAL RATE EXAMPLE** . . . In Ann Arbor, Mich., 510 E. Washington St., the weekday daytime rate is $7.00 per 24 hours, plus 7c per mile, which means that a car taken out on any weekday at 8:00 A.M.—driven 30 miles, returned before 8:00 A.M. on the next day—costs only $9.10, including gas, oil and insurance, *regardless of how many ride.* Less miles or additional miles, 7c per mile.

TRUCKS . . . *Hertz is also the world's largest truck leasing and rental organization. Trucks are available at most Hertz stations for occasional rental or on long-term lease. Call your local Hertz station for full information and complete details.*

NOTE: *To serve more cities and towns, licenses are being granted to responsible local interests to operate as part of the Hertz system. For complete information write Hertz Driv-Ur-Self System, Inc., Dept. 1109, 218 South Wabash Avenue, Chicago 4, Illinois.*

You can Rent a new Car from HERTZ as easy as A B C

SPORTS

Retired Heavyweight Champion JOE LOUIS Comes Out Of Retirement For A 10-Round Exhibition Bout At Chicago Stadium Against San Francisco's Pat Valentino.

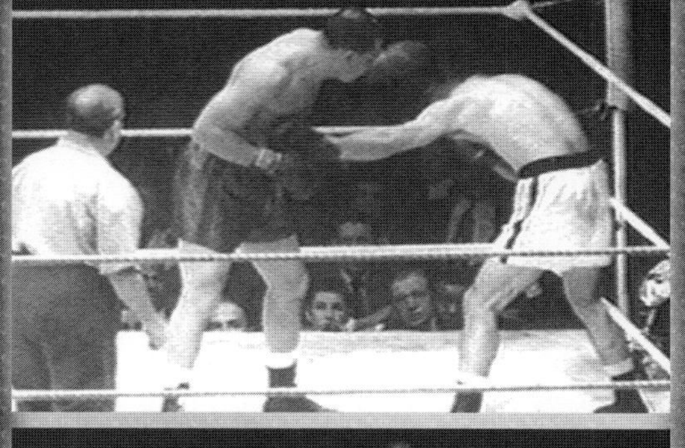

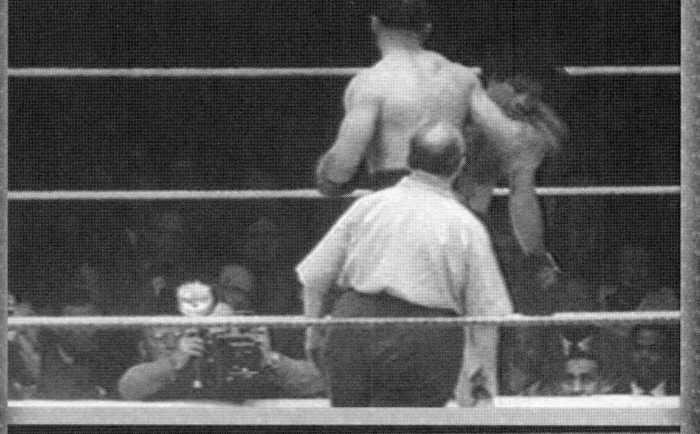

At ringside, along with 5,000 other spectators, is Ezzard Charles, who won Louis' Heavyweight crown after the Brown Bomber retired.

Still the lethal Bomber, still the methodical stalker of his opponent, the 224 pound Louis takes Valentino out in the 7th Round.

Fans are riveted as the undefeated former champ, who parlayed a pair of boxing gloves into a million bucks, proceeds to prove that he's still mighty handy with those fists.

BOXING WORLD TITLES

HEAVYWEIGHT
JOE LOUIS
Mr. Louis retires after holding the Heavyweight Champion of the World title for 12 years. Ezzard Charles wins vacated title in match with Jersey Joe Walcott.

MIDDLEWEIGHT
JAKE LA MOTTA
KO's Marcel Cerdan to win title.

WELTERWEIGHT
SUGAR RAY ROBINSON
retains title in match with Kid Gavilan.

FEATHERWEIGHT
WILLIE PEP
wins back his title in bout with Sandy Saddler.

LIGHT-HEAVYWEIGHT
JOEY MAXIM
wins title in a 15-round decision over Freddie Mills.

LIGHTWEIGHT
IKE WILLIAMS
retains title in 15-round decision over Freddie Dawson.

9 Out Of 18 Boxing Deaths This Year Are In The United States Resulting In Increased Safety Measures.

PASSINGS

French boxer **Marcel Cerdan**, 33, is killed in a plane crash enroute to the United States for a rematch against Jake La Motta.

CHICAGO'S COMISKEY PARK

sets the stage for the World Heavyweight Boxing Championship between **Ezzard Charles** and **Jersey Joe Walcott**.

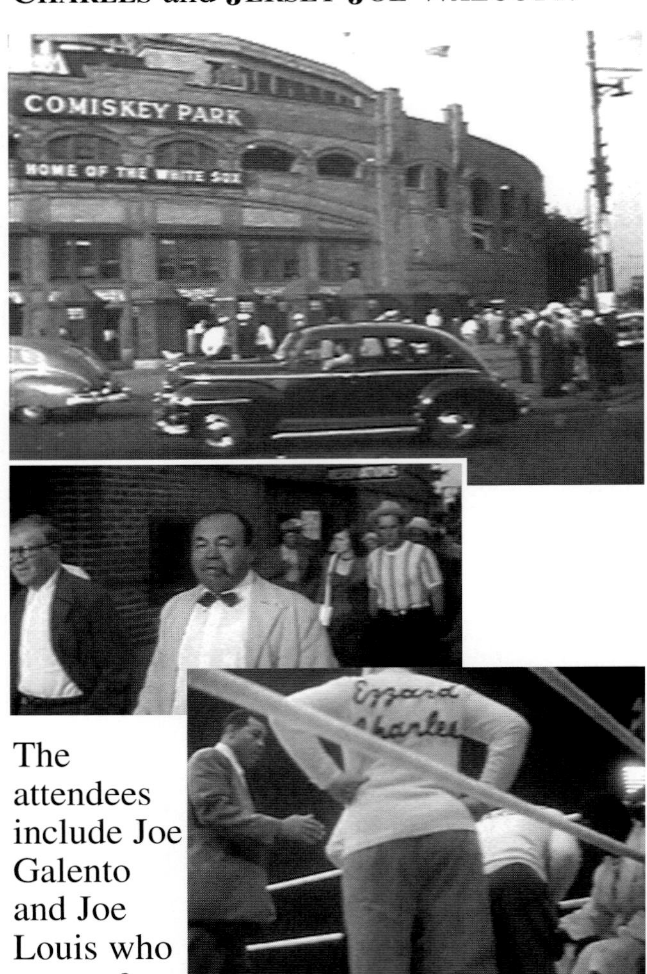

The attendees include Joe Galento and Joe Louis who says a few words to Ezzard Charles before the match begins.

Ezzard Charles Is The Winner!

1949 Baseball

CONNIE MACK Is Honored In New York

NEW YORK

Goes All Out To Honor 86-Year Old Connie Mack's 50-Year Baseball Career.

It's "Mr. Baseball's" special day and everybody turns out to make it a huge success. Thousands of fans line the motor route of the motorcade to show their appreciation to the grand old man of baseball.

Connie is given a testimonial scroll by Mayor O'Dwyer as city officials and big league stars look on.

1949 ADVERTISEMENT

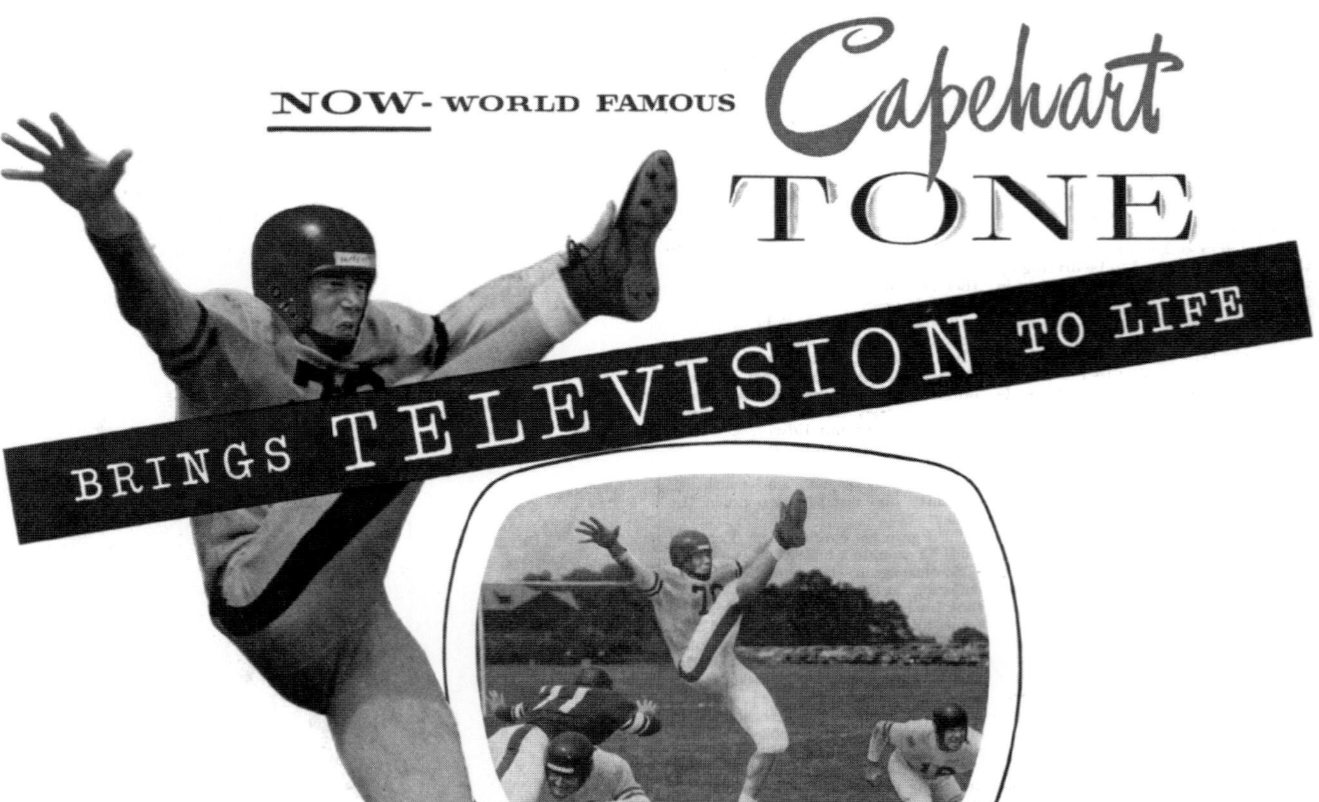

Cowhide meets pigskin with a pistol crack! Cheers, songs and band music fill the stadium! The narrator announces the names and numbers! All of the familiar sounds that put you "on the 50 yard line" are yours with Capehart's unequalled tone. You hear everything with "life-like" clarity.

The exclusive Capehart Polatron* television tube brings pictures as brilliant and clear as Capehart tone! Glare and fuzziness are eliminated. Pictures have greater depth and detail in dark or daylight, with no adjustment required.

Truly Capehart television must be *heard* and *seen*. Be sure to do *both* before you buy. *You'll be surprised at the new price range starting as low as $269.50!*

All prices slightly higher in Far West.
**T. M. Reg. Available at slight extra cost.*

CAPEHART-FARNSWORTH CORPORATION, Fort Wayne, Indiana
An IT&T Associate

THE CAPEHART Overture—*with the famous Capehart tone.* Capehart's Regency styling for those who prefer modest size with luxurious cabinetry. Rock-steady pictures—brilliant and clear—plus Capehart's unmatched fidelity of tone. Television and AM-FM service. Built-in antenna. $489.50

THE CAPEHART Symphony—*with the famous Capehart tone.* For spacious homes Capehart provides the Symphony. Television with 16 inch picture, AM-FM radio and the Capehart record changer which plays all types of records automatically. Ample record space. Built-in antenna. $795.

THE CAPEHART Serenade—*with the famous Capehart tone.* For the small home or apartment, this compact television receiver provides economy of space and investment —with a clear, brilliant image and true Capehart tonal fidelity. Built-in antenna. Modern design. Bisque finish. $309.50

THE CAPEHART French Provincial—*with the famous Capehart tone.* Fashioned from cherry with fruitwood finish. Combines the charm of Old World cabinetry with the excellence of Capehart true timbre tone. Plays all types of records automatically. AM-FM radio. Record storage compartment. $385.

Baseball

New York Yankees Defeat Brooklyn Dodgers 4-1 To Win Their 12th World Series Championship

The American League Wins All-Star Game Over National League 11-7

Most Valuable Player

National League:
Jackie Robinson (Brooklyn Dodgers)

American League:
Ted Williams (Boston Red Sox)

ROOKIE OF THE YEAR

NATIONAL LEAGUE
DON NEWCOMBE (BROOKLYN DODGERS)

AMERICAN LEAGUE
ROY SIEVERS (ST. LOUIS BROWNS)

SEASON HOME RUN KINGS

NATIONAL LEAGUE
RALPH KINER (PITTSBURGH 54 HOME RUNS)

AMERICAN LEAGUE
TED WILLIAMS (BOSTON 43 HOME RUNS)

BATTING CHAMPIONS

NATIONAL LEAGUE
JACKIE ROBINSON (BROOKLYN .342 AVERAGE)

AMERICAN LEAGUE
GEORGE KELL (DETROIT .343 AVERAGE)

- The New York Yankees Give **Joe DiMaggio** A Pay Raise, Increasing His Salary To $90,000.
- **Joe DiMaggio** Makes His 1949 Debut In Boston After Nursing An Injured Heel Hitting A Two-Run Homer In His First Game Going On To Lead The Yankees To Another World Series Win.
- **Ted Williams** Becomes Highest-Paid Player In Baseball As Boston Red Sox Sign Him For $100,000.
- A Five-Year Suspension For Switching To The Mexican League Is Lifted Against 18 Major League Players Including **Max Lanier**, **Fred Martin** And **Lou Klein**.
- The New York Giants Sign Their First Negro Players, **Hank Thompson** And **Monte Irvin**.
- Philadelphia Phillies' **Eddie Waitkus** Is Shot In A Chicago Hotel Room By A Deranged Fan.
- St. Louis Cardinals' Second Baseman **Albert "Red" Schoendienst** Establishes National League Record By Playing 39 Consecutive Games Without An Error Breaking The 38-Game Record Set In 1919 By Buck Herzog Of The Chicago Cubs.

1949

- Chicago White Sox Shortstop **Luke Appling** Sets New Major League Record By Playing His 2,154th Game In 19 Years.
- Detroit Tigers' Former Second Baseman **Charlie Gehringer** Is Only Modern Player Elected To Baseball's Hall Of Fame.
- New York Yankees Sign Recent High School Graduate **Mickey Mantle**.

Whattya' Mean He's Out!

Displeased with umpire Al Barlick's call, Philadelphia fans let loose a 15-minute barrage of bottles, cans and assorted vegetables including ripe tomatoes, forcing the players to flee to the nearest exit and forfeiture of the game.

Pitching In The Dark

Despite the National League's agreement to turn on stadium lights if afternoon games are being played after sundown, American League owners say they will only turn the lights on for the important games. Flashlight anyone?

Who You Calling A Bum!

Leo Durocher is suspended for five days for punching a fan at the Polo Grounds.

THE HEISMAN TROPHY

FOR THE OUTSTANDING FOOTBALL PLAYER OF THE YEAR is presented to LEON HART of Notre Dame

by Wilbur Jordan *(left)*, President of New York's Downtown Athletic Club.

The 255 lb. end is the first lineman to win the award in 12 years.

FOOTBALL

PHILADELPHIA EAGLES Beat LOS ANGELES RAMS 14-0 Winning National Football League Championship

NUMBER ONE NFL DRAFT CHOICE:
Chuck Bednarik Penn
Philadelphia

Associated Press National College Football Champion Choice
NOTRE DAME

Top Four College Football Teams
NOTRE DAME
OKLAHOMA
CALIFORNIA
ARMY

Football Writers Association Picks
College Football Coach of the Year
CHARLES "BUD" WILKINSON,
Oklahoma

Football Man of the Year
FRANK LEAHY,
Notre Dame Coach

President Truman among the 102,433 spectators witnessing **Army** trounce **Navy 38-0** in the biggest win of the 59-year rivalry.

Northwestern beats **California 20-14** at Rose Bowl.

On a wet, soggy field at Memorial Coliseum in Los Angeles the Philadelphia Eagles beat the Los Angeles Rams 14-0 in the National Football League Playoffs.

Despite the weather, 28,000 hearty souls show up to cheer their favorite team to victory.

And here's the winning touchdown making the Eagles champions once again.

BASKETBALL

NCAA CHAMPIONS

University Of Kentucky Beats Oklahoma State 46-36

NCAA OUTSTANDING PLAYER

Alex Groza (Kentucky)

BASKETBALL ASSOCIATION OF AMERICA (BAA) CHAMPIONS

Minneapolis Lakers Beat Washington Capitols 4-2

BAA SCORING CHAMPION

George Mikan (Minneapolis) 1,698 Points

The BAA And NBL Merge Creating The National Basketball Association.

In A Game Between Syracuse And Anderson, Referees Whistle 122 Fouls.

Philadelphia Warrior **Joe Fulks** Scores 63 Points Against The Indianapolis Jets Setting A New BAA Record For Points Scored In A Single Game.

Billiards

61-Year Old **WILLIAM HOPPE** Wins His Fifth World Three-Cushion Title Without A Loss Since 1937.

ICE HOCKEY

CALDER MEMORIAL
(Rookie Of The Year)
PENTTI LUND
New York Rangers

ROSS TROPHY
(Leading Scorer)
ROY CONACHER
Chicago

LADY BYNG MEMORIAL TROPHY
(Most Gentlemanly Player)
BILL QUACKENBUSH
Detroit

HART MEMORIAL TROPHY
(Most Valuable Player)
SID ABEL
Detroit

Toronto Maple Leafs Beat Detroit Red Wings 4-0 Winning Their Record-Breaking Third Consecutive Stanley Cup

GOLF

Ben Hogan Suffers Shattered Legs And Almost Dies From Blood Clots As A Result Of A Head-On Collision With A Bus.

The Ladies' Professional Golf Association is formed in New York headed by "Babe" Didrikson Zaharias' manager, Fred Corcoran.

Competing in the 49th National Women's Amateur Championship, 15-year old Marlene Bauer is youngest contender to reach the semifinals.

CHAMPIONS

MASTERS
Sam Snead
($10,000 purse)

U.S. AMATEUR
Charles R. Coe

U.S. OPEN
MEN: **Cary Middlecoff**
WOMEN: **Louise Suggs**

PROFESSIONAL GOLFERS
Sam Snead
(Also leading money winner)

BRITISH OPEN
Bobby Locke

Jockey *Steve Brooks* Rides PONDER To Kentucky Derby Win.

17-Year Old *Willie Shoemaker* Wins His First Race And Is Paid $10.

CAPOT Ridden By *T. Atkinson* Wins The Preakness And Belmont Stakes And Is Chosen "Horse Of The Year."

ICE SKATING

James E. Sullivan Memorial Trophy

Awarded For Outstanding Sportsmanship

Dick Button
Skating

World Figure Skating Championship	
Men:	Dick Button (U.S.)
Women:	Alena Vrzanova (Czechoslovakia)

U.S. National	
Men:	Dick Button
Women:	Yvonne Sherman

Canadian National	
Men:	Roger Wickson
Women:	Suzanne Morrow

Bowling

AMERICAN BOWLING CONGRESS CHAMPIONS	
All Events:	John Small
Singles:	Bernard Rusche

WOMEN'S INTERNATIONAL BOWLING CONGRESS CHAMPIONS	
All Events:	Cecilia Winandy
Singles:	Clara Mataya

1949 ADVERTISEMENT

1949

TENNIS

CHAMPIONS

U.S. Open

Men: Poncho Gonzales (over F. R. Schroeder, Jr.)
Women: Margaret Osborne du Pont (over Doris Hart)

U.S. Professional Tennis

Singles: Bobby Riggs
Doubles: Don Budge & Frank Kovacs

Wimbledon

Men: Ted Schroeder (over Jaroslav Drobny)
Women: Louise Brough (over Margaret Osborne du Pont)

Davis Cup

U.S. Beats Australia 4-1.

Czech Tennis Pros Jaroslav Drobny And Vladimir Cernik Defect In Geneva.

SOMETHING TO BARK ABOUT!

THE TOP DOG AT THE WESTMINSTER KENNEL CLUB SHOW HELD AT MADISON SQUARE GARDEN IS MR. & MRS. JOHN P. WAGNER'S BOXER CHAMPION MAZELAINE'S ZAZARAC BRANDY.

ATHLETE OF THE YEAR

Male
LEON HART
(Football)

Female
MARLENE BAUER
(Golf)

CHESS

WORLD CHESS CHAMPIONSHIP

Mikhail Botvinnik
USSR

INTERNATIONAL CHESS MASTERS TOURNAMENT WINNER

Nicholas Rossolimo
France

HANDBALL

VICTOR HERSHKOWITZ of Brooklyn, New York wins the A.A.U. Four-Wall Championship against current champion Gus Lewis becoming the first Four-Wall champion to also hold the One-Wall Singles Title.

CAR RACING

INDIANAPOLIS 500 WINNER

BILL HOLLAND driving Blue Crown Special at average speed of 121 M.P.H. Holland collects $51,575 in winnings.

WINSTON CUP CHAMP

RED BYRON

WRESTLING

NATIONAL CHAMPIONS U.S. AMATEUR ATHLETIC UNION TEAM CROWN

Iowa State Teachers College

NATIONAL COLLEGIATE ATHLETIC ASSOCIATION TITLE

Oklahoma A&M
(16th time in 19 years)

FAMOUS BIRTHS

Ahmad Rashad
•
George Foreman
•
Bruce Jenner
•
Scott Hamilton

1949 WAS A GREAT YEAR, BUT...